Reflecting on 30 Years of Nursing Leadership: 1975–2005

Sister Rosemary Donley, SC, PhD, APRN, BC, FAAN

Books Published by the Honor Society of Nursing, Sigma Theta Tau International

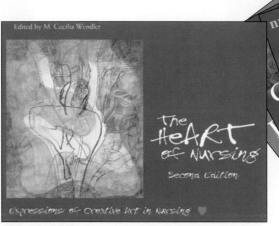

The HeART of Nursing: Expressions of Creative Art in Nursing, Second Edition, Wendler, 2005.

nurseAdvance Collection.
(Topic-specific collections of honor society published journal articles.) Topics offered are: Implementing Evidence-Based Nursing, Women's Health Nursing, Leadership and Mentoring in Nursing, Pediatric Nursing, Maternal Health Nursing, Gerontological Nursing, Oncology Nursing, Psychiatric-Mental Health Nursing, and Women's Health Nursing. 2005.

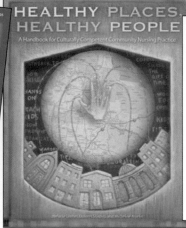

Healthy Places, Healthy People, Melanie Dreher, RN, PhD, FAAN, Dolores Shapiro, RN, PhD, Micheline Asselin, RN, MSN, MPA, CHPN, 2005.

Reflecting on Thirty Years of Nursing Leadership, Donley, 2005.

Technological Competency as Caring in Nursing, Locsin, 2005.

Making a Difference: Stories from the Point of Care, Volume 2, Hudacek, 2005.

A Daybook for Nurses: Making a Difference Each Day, Hudacek, 2004.

Making a Difference: Stories from the Point of Care, Volume 1, Hudacek, 2004.

Pivotal Moments in Nursing: Leaders Who Changed the Path of a Profession, Houser and Player, 2004.

Building and Managing a Career in Nursing: Strategies for Advancing Your Career, Miller, 2003.

Collaboration for the Promotion of Nursing, Briggs, Merk, and Mitchell, 2003.

Ordinary People, Extraordinary Lives: The Stories of Nurses, Smeltzer and Vlasses, 2003.

Stories of Family Caregiving: Reconsideration of Theory, Literature, and Life, Poirier and Ayres, 2002.

As We See Ourselves: Jewish Women in Nursing, Benson, 2001.

Cadet Nurse Stories: The Call for and Response of Women During World War II, Perry and Robinson, 2001.

Creating Responsive Solutions to Healthcare Change, McCullough, 2001.

Nurses' Moral Practice: Investing and Discounting Self, Kelly, 2000.

Nursing and Philanthropy: An Energizing Metaphor for the 21st Century, McBride, 2000.

Gerontological Nursing Issues for the 21st Century, Gueldner and Poon, 1999.

The Roy Adaptation Model-Based Research: 25 Years of Contributions to Nursing Science, Boston Based Adaptation Research in Nursing Society, 1999.

The Adventurous Years: Leaders in Action 1973-1999, Henderson, 1998.

Immigrant Women and Their Health: An Olive Paper, Ibrahim Meleis, Lipson,Muecke and Smith, 1998.

The Neuman Systems Model and Nursing Education: Teaching Strategies and Outcomes, Lowry, 1998.

The Image Editors: Mind, Spirit, and Voice, Hamilton, 1997.

The Language of Nursing Theory and Metatheory, King and Fawcett, 1997.

Virginia Avenel Henderson: Signature for Nursing, Hermann, 1997.

For more information and to order these books from the Honor Society of Nursing, Sigma Theta Tau International, visit the honor society's Web site at www.nursingsociety.org/publications. Or go to www.nursingknowledge.org/stti/books, the Web site of Nursing Knowledge International, the honor society's sales and distribution division, or call 1.888.NKI.4.YOU (U.S. and Canada) or +1.317.634.8171 (Outside U.S. and Canada).

Reflecting on 30 Years of Nursing Leadership: 1975–2005

Sister Rosemary Donley, SC, PhD, APRN, BC, FAAN

Sigma Theta Tau International
Honor Society of Nursing®

Sigma Theta Tau International

Editor-in-Chief: Jeff Burnham
Acquisitions Editor: Fay L. Bower, RN, DNSc, FAAN
Editors: Carla Hall and Jane Palmer
Editorial Team: Margie Wilson, Melody Jones, James E. Mattson

Art Direction by: James E. Mattson
Cover Design by: Rebecca Harmon
Production Design and Typesetting by: Rebecca Harmon

Printed in the United States of America
Printing and Binding by: V.G. Reed & Sons

Sigma Theta Tau International
550 West North Street
Indianapolis, IN 46202 USA

Visit our Web site at **www.nursingknowledge.org/STTI/books** for more information on our books.

05   06   07   08 / 9   8   7   6   5   4   3   2   1

Dedication

This book is dedicated to the memory of Nell J. Watts
in recognition of her many years of visionary leadership
of Sigma Theta Tau International.

Acknowledgements

I AM GRATEFUL TO THE members of the Sigma Theta Tau International board of directors, to Nancy Dickenson-Hazard, to Fay Bower, and to the wonderful editorial staff of the society, particularly Jeff Burnham, Carla Hall, and Jane Palmer for their decision to celebrate the 30-year history of *Reflections* and for the encouragement and support they have shown to me as I have reflected on its meaning to the society and to the discipline of nursing.

About the Author

SR. ROSEMARY DONLEY, SC, PhD, APRN, BC, FAAN, currently an ordinary professor with The Catholic University of America (CUA), was formerly an executive vice president and a dean of nursing for CUA. Her many professional experiences include being a Robert Wood Johnson Health Policy Fellow, a member of the Institute of Medicine, a board member of the Catholic Health Association, a board member of the Nursing Economics Foundation, and past president of The Honor Society of Nursing, Sigma Theta Tau International and the National League for Nursing. Sr. Donley has been an active member of the honor society for 40 years.

Contents

Foreword

FOR THE BETTER PART of 12 years, I have regularly communicated with members of the Honor Society of Nursing, Sigma Theta Tau International through the pages of *Reflections on Nursing Leadership (RNL)*. Usually these editorials, or "notes" as I have called them, relate to the issue's quarterly theme.

Often, I begin these notes by drawing upon a family experience. I do this for two reasons: People identify with personal stories and it helps get my creative juices flowing. Family is very important to me, so when I start writing about a family event or tradition that relates in some way to *RNL's* current editorial focus, the words just seem to flow a whole lot easier.

Reflections on Nursing Leadership is all about family—our professional family. Because open communication is so important to caring, healthy families, the leaders of the honor society had the foresight in 1975 to publish a newsletter they called *Reflections*. The purpose was to provide "a channel of communications for national officers, national committees, and chapters for newsworthy information of national interest."

CEO Nancy Dickenson-Hazard helping celebrate the 30th anniversary of
Reflections on Nursing Leadership.

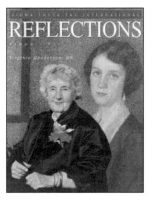
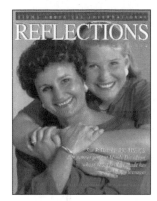
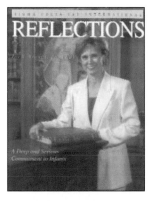

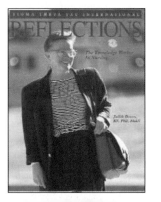

Fast forward 30 years. ... The society's world is no longer just national in scope. It has been international for 20 years, and *Reflections* and its namesake, *Reflections on Nursing Leadership,* have contributed greatly to this global scope. In addition to facilitating better communication within a professional family—then limited to the US—this publication helped us lift our myopic gaze beyond US borders and begin seeing nurses and nursing around the world better and with more clarity and improved understanding. With time, the magazine's purpose became more focused, "to communicate nurses' contributions and relevance to the health of people worldwide."

Looking back, from this 30-year vantage point, we can readily see the progress in publishing the news and perspectives of our global family. Recent headway to publish *Reflections on Nursing Leadership* online via the Web enables quicker communication with even the most distant and remote family members and significantly expands the information, articles, and features that reach them. As *Reflections on Nursing Leadership* continues to evolve, its purposes will remain steady: to improve family communication, to tell the stories of nurses' contributions to global health, and to celebrate the art and science of the profession.

Happy Birthday *Reflections on Nursing Leadership,* from your family of nurse leaders and scholars from around the world! May you have many more!

Nancy Dickenson-Hazard, RN, MSN, FAAN
Chief Executive Officer
The Honor Society of Nursing, Sigma Theta Tau International

Preface

A S I REFLECT ON THE PAST 5 years since coming to the Honor Society of Nursing, Sigma Theta Tau International, one of the things that most stands out in my mind is the opportunity I have had to be involved with the publication of the honor society's member newsmagazine, *Reflections on Nursing Leadership (RNL)*. I have been so impressed by the consistent excellence, professionalism, commitment, and dedication of the honor society's leaders, members, and staff that are exemplified in the pages of each issue. I have come to see that *RNL* is a reflection of a high level of excellence, professionalism, commitment, and dedication, and it has been for the past 30 years since its humble beginnings as a four-page, one-color newsletter called *Reflections*.

We can thank the visionary leadership of Sr. Rosemary Donley, president of Sigma Theta Tau from 1975 to 1981, and Nell J. Watts, Sigma Theta Tau's executive officer from 1974 to 1993, for their decision 30 years ago to launch a member newsletter to facilitate communication between the honor society's headquarters, members, and chapters. The evolution and growth of *Reflections* from a newsletter into an award-winning, full-color newsmagazine over the past 30 years has mirrored the

evolution and growth of the honor society itself, from a national to a global organization, increasing its membership by almost tenfold over those 3 decades. It only seemed fitting, then, that Sr. Donley author this book chronicling the past three decades of the honor society through the pages of *Reflections*.

I have observed that the development and publication of each quarterly issue of *RNL* is truly a collaborative affair, involving honor society leaders, members, and staff from every level of the organization. We have what we call an "all-staff review" of each issue, in which page proofs of the issue are placed in the board-room at honor society headquarters, and all staff members are invited to review the galley proofs before the magazine is sent to the printer. Every issue ends up being better than it would otherwise have been because of this process.

In 1991, Nell Watts hired a professional journalist named Julie Goldsmith as the first staff editor of *Reflections* to help transform the newsletter into a news-magazine. Under Goldsmith's editorship from 1991 to 2000, the newsmagazine grew in editorial and production quality, receiving accolades from journalism groups and a Media Award from the American Academy of Nursing. This tradition of excellence continued under the current editor, James Mattson, beginning in 2000. Jim brought to *RNL* a rare combination of both editorial and graphic design skills, which have resulted in continued improvements in the quality. In 2004 and 2005 alone, Jim received seven prestigious journalism awards for editorial and design excellence, including yet another Media Award from the American Academy of Nursing in 2005.

Over the past 5 years, I have often heard honor society leaders, members, and staff remark that each issue of *Reflections on Nursing Leadership* just seems to be better than the last—continuous quality improvement. I am a child of the 1960s who came of age with The Beatles, so whenever I hear such a comment I can't help but think of The Beatles singing "It's Getting Better All the Time." That's how I think of the honor society and its newsmagazine.

It's getting better all the time!

Jeff Burnham
Editor-in-Chief
Sigma Theta Tau International

Introduction

T HE INVITATION TO WRITE a history of *Reflections* came shortly before the death of Nell J. Watts, the first executive officer of Sigma Theta Tau International. What a wonderful memorial, I thought, recalling our discussions in 1974 about beginning a newsletter. Nell Watts believed that professional organizations were communication entities. Before she became the executive officer, members and chapter officers complained about inadequate communication with the national organization. *Reflections* became part of a larger strategy to create a modern organization, to enhance networking and to weave a mosaic that linked nurse scholars to each other and to the national organization. We invested energy in naming the newsletter, playing with the word *Image,* the title of Sigma Theta Tau International's scholarly journal in the 1970s (now called *Journal of Nursing Scholarship*). *Reflections* would be a companion to *Image.* It would not duplicate or replicate its work, but it would encourage and publicize research opportunities, share scholarly work, acquaint members with opportunities to present their research and theoretical formulations, and address obstacles to developing careers as nurse scholars. We

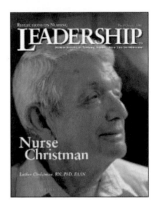

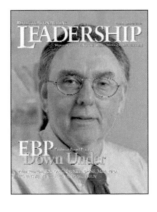

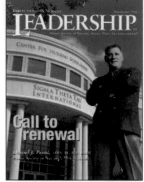
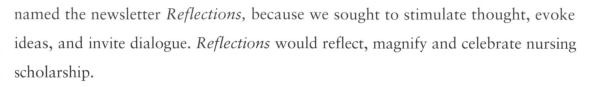

named the newsletter *Reflections*, because we sought to stimulate thought, evoke ideas, and invite dialogue. *Reflections* would reflect, magnify and celebrate nursing scholarship.

It has been a privilege to look back, like Alice, through the reflection that the newsletter-magazine cast as Sigma Theta Tau International became the premier scholarly society in the world. It was an exciting, humbling and intellectually stimulating experience to read each issue of *Reflections*.

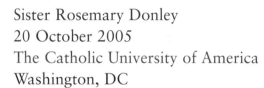

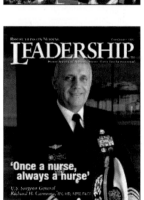

Sister Rosemary Donley
20 October 2005
The Catholic University of America
Washington, DC

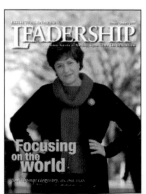

The Beginnings: 1975–1989

THIRTY YEARS is just a wisp of time or an eternity, depending upon which side of the generation gap one stands. For professional nursing in general and for Sigma Theta Tau in particular, it was a time when great minds and great leaders were generating important nursing scholarship and research; building and designing new nursing schools and degree programs; and taking charge at high levels in government, hospitals, colleges and universities, and in nearly every aspect of healthcare (Houser & Player, 2004).

To gain some perspective of what 30 years ago looked like for many of us, consider these modern, worldwide milestones:

Thirty Years Ago …

- The first "personal computer," the IBM 5100, was launched. It weighed 50 pounds and came with a price tag of just under USD $20,000 for 64 kilobytes

of memory and compatibility with two different programming languages, BASIC and APL (Blinkenlights Archaeological Institute, 1999-2002; IBM, n.d).

- The world's population was 4 billion (2005 population is just over 6.4 billion) (Wikipedia, 2005b).

- The Nobel Prize in Medicine was awarded to a team for "describing how tumor viruses act on the genetic material of the cell" (Wikipedia, 2005a).

- The Biomedicus Bio-Pump (centrifugal) was introduced for clinical application (Vinas, 1999).

- The first computerized axial tomography ("CAT-scanner") was introduced (Vinas, 1999).

- Smallpox was almost eradicated (World Health Organization, 2005), and HIV/AIDS was unheard of (World Health Organization, 2003).

The honor society was just a fraction of the size it would later grow to with 15,200 active members (June 2005 rolls show 128,522 active members) in 65 chapters (2005 numbers show 430 chapters), but Sigma Theta Tau leadership needed a way to communicate easily and effectively with this growing and far-reaching membership base.

Thus, the first issue of *Reflections* appeared on 15 March 1975 as a modest, four-page, black and white newsletter. The lead story announced the national council of Sigma Theta Tau had launched a new channel of communication

	1975	**2005**
Active Members	15,200	128,522
Number of Chapters	65	430

The first issue of *Reflections* appeared on 15 March 1975 as a modest, four-page, black and white newsletter.

between national officers and committees, chapters, and members. While the early issues lacked color and sophistication, the dominant values of Sigma Theta Tau—promotion of research and recognition of scholarly achievement—were emphasized. These topics became the template for the newsletter, and *Reflections* became a mode for increasing the visibility of the organization and its national officers, committees, and programs.

At first, only chapter and national programs such as research conferences and biennial meetings were promoted in *Reflections*. Chapter members used it to report news and invite participation in programs and research conferences. Very quickly, however, members began contributing to *Reflections*, proudly proclaiming the completion of their doctoral studies and announcing their promotions, publications, and awards—this section would eventually become known as "Noteworthy."

Themes

Several themes are evident in the early years of *Reflections*. In the 1970s, writers described the development of Sigma Theta Tau as a force in nursing. Part member newsletter and part community bulletin board, *Reflections* became the voice of members and a vehicle for disseminating information about research, scholarship, and professional advancement.

> Part member newsletter and part community bulletin board, *Reflections* became the voice of members and a vehicle for disseminating information about research, scholarship, and professional advancement.

Sigma Theta Tau—A Significant and Future-Oriented Organization

In the early years, each volume of *Reflections* carried a message from the president. In the inaugural issue, Sr. Rosemary Donley discussed the meaning and responsibility of membership in Sigma Theta Tau.

President Donley noted that the members of Sigma Theta Tau were leaders, academically talented, and the most educated of the professional nursing force. The thrust of her remarks was that membership was both an honor and a responsibility. This idea would be developed into the Avenues of Action theme of the 23rd Biennial Convention held in 1975 in Houston, Texas.

During the meeting, delegates engaged in an interactive process to identify and discuss ways to address the gaps in education, practice, and research that blocked the actualization of nursing as a science and limited access to healthcare. At the end of the 1975 meeting, delegates embraced a proactive agenda to identify and then close the gaps in nursing education, practice, and research in the communities where they lived and worked.

The 1975 Biennial Convention in Texas and the adoption of the Avenues of Action agenda were turning points in the organization's history. One important

Sr. Rosemary Donley.

and enduring structure, the Educational Development Committee (EDC), which later became the Regional Chapter Coordinating Committee, was formed at the meeting to provide a framework for engaging chapters and members in national and regional programming efforts. The first members were appointed to represent regions of the country: Margaret Jacobson, Western region; Lily Larson, Plains; Janet Brown, Northeast; Patricia Chamings, South; Lillian Pierce, Great Lakes; and Rebecca Markel, Midwest. Markel chaired the committee. The Avenues of Action theme was evident in *Reflections* as headlines announced both "Members in Action" and "Chapters in Action."

The EDC worked locally and regionally with members and chapters in the development of programs related to the theme. This was the first time the national organization had become involved in direct support of chapter activities. Each issue of *Reflections* included a report of local expressions of nursing scholarship and research. This theme nourished the organization until 1979 when the delegates to the 25th Biennial Convention in Seattle adopted a new emphasis: Leadership in Action—Visible, Viable, Vital. Here, keynote speaker Margretta Madden Styles identified the leadership qualities of career commitment, assertiveness, accountability, professional trust, and goal orientation.

Extension and expansion of Sigma Theta Tau became major focuses in the 1970s. "Seventy six chapters in 1976" became the impetus for chapter development around the nation. Addressing organizational structures and traditions, marketing the organization at national meetings, and clarifying the process of honor society formation were constitutive elements in this process. Executive Officer Nell Watts, EDC member Lily Larson, and national officers and committee members promulgated the importance of having a Sigma Theta Tau chapter on each college and university campus. Member engagement and chapter involvement were critical to closing the gaps in education, practice, and research. However, there was another factor that facilitated chapter engagement and growth: At the biennial meeting in Texas, delegates voted to give the national organization the authority to collect national and chapter dues. Chapter leaders received their funds and a list of active members from the staff of the national organization. Soon, Watts managed the computerization of the mailing list for ease of use and upkeep.

Reflections/November/December, 1979　　　　　　　　　　　Page 5

At The Convention

Leadership Luncheon

Marci Catanzaro

House of Delegates

Left to right: Elizabeth McWilliams Miller, Josephine Dolan, Rebecca Markel, Jean McKinley and Sr. Rosemary Donley.

Nell Watts

Left to right seated: Elizabeth McWilliams Miller, Marie Hippensteel Lingeman and Edith Moore Copeland, founders, and Josephine Dolan, standing.

Left to right: Kitty Smith, Jean McKinley, Patricia Hayes, Kathryn Schweer, and John Pitcherale.

Luther Christman　　Sr. Rosemary with Lee Conant

Margretta Styles

Carol Lindeman

Lucie Kelly

Maureen Niland

Mary Davis

Registration Desk

Left to right: Mary Kelly, Mullane and Sr. Rosemary Donley

Nell J. Watts, executive officer of Sigma Theta Tau from 1974 to 1993.

Simplifying chapter dues collection and providing access to an accurate mailing list gave the chapter officers more time and the funds to engage in program development and cultivation of new members. Members paid $2 a year in national dues. Watts proudly informed the membership at the end of 1978 that the organization was healthy and growing, with 26,500 active members in 94 chapters. The first chapter outside the continental US was chartered at the University of Hawaii. There was international support for scholarly nursing and membership commitment for a new building and a capital fund for nursing research. Between 1976 and 1977, there was an increase in:

- membership—41%

- contribution to research—82%

- number of chapters—22%

- manuscripts for publication in *Image* (later to be renamed *Image: Journal of Nursing Scholarship*, then *Journal of Nursing Scholarship*)—85%

In 1975, the leaders of Sigma Theta Tau expanded the research focus by organizing research conferences and presentations at the conventions of the National League for Nursing (NLN) and American Nurses Association (ANA). They also designed an exhibit booth for the NLN and ANA meetings. The first Sigma Theta Tau booth, booth 911, was unveiled at the NLN convention in New Orleans, LA, in May 1975. By 1979, Sigma Theta Tau had hosted a series of meetings at ANA and NLN conventions. The meetings helped advance the Sigma Theta Tau nursing scholarship and research agenda and increased communication with and among members. At these meetings, Watts led discussions about ways Sigma Theta Tau could make a difference in nursing and in individual nurses' professional lives. Eventually, these meetings would evolve into the annual Sigma Theta Tau International Research Congress, which has grown to nearly 1,000 attendees annually.

In her honor society vision presented at the 24th Biennial Convention in Washington, DC, President Donley (1978) called Sigma Theta Tau a unique place to be.

> Envision a day when Sigma Theta Tau has a center for nursing research, a program which supports scholars during a sabbatical year, a fellowship program which engages students of nursing in creative leadership activity, a building which houses a museum of nursing history, as well as a film and publication center. ... Sigma Theta Tau is an organization which brings together the most gifted and educated among the nursing profession. Consequently Sigma Theta Tau can be confident of the ability of its members to demonstrate leadership roles in nursing and health care systems (p. 1).

Evidence-based practice was not in the vocabulary of nurses and physicians in the 1970s. Yet there was a repeated emphasis on the importance of applying research to practice.

Promoting Research and Scholarship

In March 1976, a presentation given by Myrtle Aydelotte, director and professor of nursing at the University of Iowa, as well as Sigma Theta Tau past president, was highlighted. She defined clinical research as "The extension of coherent knowledge that enables the practitioner to practice more effectively. Clinical nursing research requires the use of the health care delivery system as its laboratory" (p.4). Evidence-based practice was not in the vocabulary of nurses and physicians in the 1970s. Yet there was a repeated emphasis on the importance of applying research to practice. For instance, the keynote speaker at the 1977 Biennial Convention, Congresswoman Martha Keyes, commended and challenged members on their Avenues of Action when she urged nurses to enact their role in policy making as well as in professional health care delivery.

Leadership in Action

In the fall of 1978, President Donley and Carol Lindeman, who would succeed Sr. Donley as Sigma Theta Tau president in 1981, were invited to testify at the National Conference on Health Research Principles held at the National Institutes of Health. Sr. Donley argued for research that focused on the special needs of minorities, the aged, and the chronically disabled and noted that professional nurses represented an untapped resource for research into health services. Lindeman urged that research dollars be stretched across all components of a healthcare model. She recommended multidisciplinary, behavioral, and biological research.

It was obvious to leaders and members of Sigma Theta Tau that more nurses needed to be educated and supported in developing research agendas and scholarly careers.

> In 1934, Sigma Theta Tau established a research fund to (1) foster development of the scientific attitude in relation to nursing problems, (2) to give financial aid in the execution of research in this field, and (3) to help awaken nurses to the fact that there is a field for research in nursing.
>
> More recently, the National Council reiterated the society's support for research and the intent "to expand the support for discovery of new nursing knowledge." In 1976, a research endowment fund was initiated to provide expanded support for nursing research at a time when other available funding sources appeared to be decreasing. The national organization chose to initiate the fund with contributions from members prior to approaching non-member contributors. The outstanding membership support for this fund has been reassuring. Ten percent of renewing members have contributed and built the fund to more than $40,000 (Watts, 1979, p.2).

The research grant program was promoted in *Reflections* by the publication of deadlines, pictures, and biographies of research award recipients, as well as follow-up reports of awardees' progress. Grantees were frequently invited to present their work at research sessions at NLN and ANA meetings. These presentations were reported in the newsletter. Activities to promote research were faithfully published

Alice Crist Malone, MA, received the first known research grant from STT for $600 in 1936. She studied how to measure achievement in nursing based upon new curriculum objectives.

in *Reflections*. Space was also allocated to chapter research programs and research awards. Later, chapter calendars became regular features in *Reflections*. These calendars gave members an opportunity to submit research abstracts for review and the opportunity to present their work to peers and colleagues.

The first list of nurse members who earned doctorates was published in *Reflections* in 1976. The listing included the dissertation title, the degree earned, and the school awarding the degree. This recognition of members' achievements was important. Each year, at least one page of *Reflections* was devoted to recognizing academic achievement. Recognition encouraged members to see their names in print and provided a source of national data about emerging nurse scholars for deans and vice presidents of nursing. In 1981, a listing of schools of nursing that offered doctoral degrees was published, which also documented the growth of doctoral study in the US.

At the end of 1978, it was announced in *Reflections* that the research committee, under the leadership of Ruth Barnard, had completed its work on the Research Depository. Members could order the publication from headquarters. In 1979, a column on nursing research became a regular feature in *Reflections*.

In March 1976, only five of the Sigma Theta Tau founders were still living. Fortunately, their stories were recorded, as Sr. Donley traveled across the country to meet these outstanding women and to hear the story of the origins of the Honor Society of Nursing, Sigma Theta Tau International. These interviews were a prelude to the establishment of awards named for the founders and their mentor, Ethel Palmer Clarke. In 1975, the national council of Sigma Theta Tau established the Founders Awards. Named after the six students who created the society at the Indiana University Training School for Nurses, these prestigious awards were given for the first time at the 24th Biennial Convention in Washington, DC, in 1977. They are given each biennium to honor contemporary nurse leaders whose lives and actions exemplify the goals of the honor society.

As part of its program to recognize achievement and scholarship, Sigma Theta Tau leaders collaborated with the National Library of Medicine in the development of a series of videotapes that highlighted the lives and careers of distinguished leaders in nursing. In the interviews, past President Ruth Hepler interviewed Lucile Petry Leone. Anna Coles, dean of Howard University School of Nursing, interviewed Mabel (Keaton) Staupers. The premier showing of the videotape series "Beyond Alpha" and Sr. Donley's interviews with the founders of Sigma Theta Tau were showcased in *Reflections*.

A series of regional programs around scholarly themes was inaugurated by Sigma Theta Tau and the EDC. The writers' seminars were the first such programs. Designed to assist members in grant writing and writing for publication, the 140 members (24 chapters in 11 states) heard Margretta Madden Styles, dean of the University of California at San Francisco, say, "The primary reason to publish is that the future of the profession depends upon it" (Writers' seminar, 1978, p. 8). The first program was pilot tested in Burlingame, CA, in March 1978.

Becoming International

Arranged to coincide with the International Congress of Nursing (ICN) meeting in Tokyo, Japan, in June 1977, the honor society's first international meeting was a very exciting venture into the world of scholarship. The meeting explored international cooperation to promote scholarly nursing. This first Sigma Theta Tau international meeting, in Budokan Hall in Tokyo, was attended by nurses from 11 countries and 15 US states. Participants recommended that Sigma Theta Tau:

- Host meetings and research conferences at future ICN meetings;

- Develop an international column in *Reflections*; and

- Explore international cooperation for the promotion of scholarly nursing exchange of international nursing students and the development of "sister" relationships between Sigma Theta Tau chapters and international schools of nursing.

The group also asked that names of Sigma Theta Tau members be shared within the country and that chapters be invited to induct eligible international students into the society while still in school in the US. Rozella Schlotfeldt, Anne Zimmerman, and Madeleine Leininger participated in the first international Sigma Theta Tau meeting along with Sr. Donley and Nell Watts.

The first international column appeared in the March-April 1978 issue of *Reflections*.

Philanthropy Comes Alive

Another first in the history of Sigma Theta Tau might have been lost if it were not for *Reflections*. In the January-March 1977 issue, the society's entry into fund raising was quietly announced. One thousand members responded to a line item on the dues renewal form that year and contributed to the first capital research fund. As reported in *Reflections*, by January 1978, 1,600 members had contributed to this fund. Nell Watts noted in 1979 that approximately 10% of active members had contributed to the research fund each year. Sigma Theta Tau members played a significant role in the development of the Capital Research Fund. Their gifts enabled more nurses to begin research careers.

This low-key, quiet method of fund raising would become very important when the society launched a major capital campaign to build the Center for Nursing Scholarship. The first gift to what would become the major fund-raising effort of Sigma Theta Tau was reported in *Reflections*. Lily Larson, EDC member and former national second vice president, made the first gift of $100 to the newly established Headquarters Fund.

"Sigma Theta Tau is about the important business of scholarship … cultivating the development of nursing science and fostering and nurturing nurse scholars." Sr. Rosemary Donley, 1980.

The Business of Sigma Theta Tau

Speaking at the 24th Biennial Convention in Washington, DC, in 1977, President Donley addressed the mission of the society, reminding delegates that the purpose of Sigma Theta Tau was not to amass resources, talented individuals, prestigious schools, and research funds. Instead, Donley stated, "Sigma Theta Tau is about the important business of scholarship … cultivating the development of nursing science and fostering and nurturing nurse scholars."

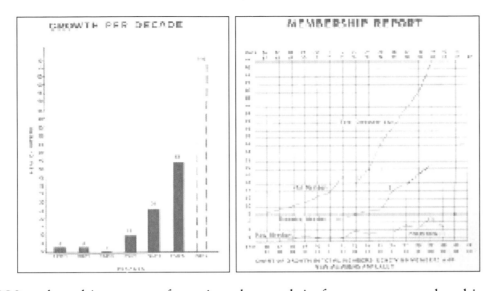

The 1980s ushered in an era of continued growth in four areas: membership, chapters, programs, and scholarship and research. By 1982, there were 161 chapters and 65,000 members. In the January-February 1982 issue of *Reflections*, a profile of the society's membership was published: 63% had master's or higher degrees; 67% were less than 40 years of age; 24% were staff nurses; 24% were faculty; 21% served as administrators, 10% were advanced practice nurses; 73% worked full time, and 43% worked in hospitals.

Building the Center for Nursing Scholarship

The building fund contained $60,960; the research fund contained $113,145. The year was 1981.

Ten-Year Plan

After a 10-year plan was adopted at the 26th Biennial Convention in Minneapolis, MN, in 1981, the goals were disseminated, updated, evaluated, and kept before the members in *Reflections*, presenting the plan as a blueprint for excellence. True to the mission, the plan focused on scholarship and was directed toward resource development, knowledge expansion, and knowledge utilization.

The 10-year plan was built on the premise that the health status of people can be improved by enhancing the knowledge base of nursing. It addressed three audiences: the community of nurses, the public, and the body of knowledge itself.

In the 1980s, *Reflections* became the vehicle for increasing awareness of the scholarly activity of members and for promoting fund raising for the research and building funds.

> The 10-year plan was built on the premise that the health status of people can be improved by enhancing the knowledge base of nursing.

Voices Are Heard

Because the Center for Nursing Scholarship was to be by, for, and about nurses, Sigma Theta Tau leadership solicited members' opinions to guide architects as they drafted plans for the new building. Six hundred members completed and returned their surveys. The results were published in *Reflections*. Seventy-five percent of the respondents considered Sigma Theta Tau publications to be the most valuable member benefit; 83% of the respondents believed the society was well-known as a scholarly organization, and 82% believed Sigma Theta Tau provided them with an opportunity for scholarly growth. In addition, chapter programs and grant-writing programs (the writers' seminars) were most highly ranked.

Chapter development continued to be a major activity. Chapter installations and the growth of Sigma Theta Tau in the academic nursing community in the US and around the world were reported in *Reflections*.

Mary Tolle Wright, the last living founder of Sigma Theta Tau, paid tribute to her departed colleague, Elizabeth Russell Belford, during the 26th Biennial Convention in 1981. Here, Carol Lindeman assumed the presidency of the society, succeeding Sr. Donley, who had led the organization since 1975. Lucie Young Kelly was elected president-elect. In her presidential speech, Lindeman challenged the delegates to be "scholars in action."

The major work of the 1981 convention was the adoption of the 10-year plan; however, other important organizational business conducted by the delegates was reported in *Reflections*. The EDC (Educational Development Committee) became the Regional Chapter Coordinating Committee, and delegates increased the national annual renewal fee from $5 to $10.

Lindeman, president from 1981-1983, conceptualized Sigma Theta Tau as a multi-imaged society that promoted nursing as a professional practice of great social

significance. She saw members as an active, committed group of sophisticated nurses who know what to do and how to go about doing it.

Turning 60

Image Makers: Richness in Diversity became the theme of the 27th Biennial Convention in Boston in 1983. Here, 1,200 honor society members celebrated the 60th anniversary of Sigma Theta Tau.

Lucie Young Kelly became president of Sigma Theta Tau at the end of the Boston meeting in 1983. In her presidential address, she highlighted the role of image makers in communicating to the public. She also focused on mentoring and encouraged individuals and chapters to become mentors. The following year, mentor chapters had been identified and a chapter mentoring program was launched. During the Kelly presidency, speakers at regional assemblies expressed image-making themes and addressed Patterns of Success in Nursing. Writers' workshops were also a major programmatic thrust in the early 1980s.

During the Kelly presidency, a presidential chain was designed. Since then, this symbol of office has been worn by all Sigma Theta Tau International presidents.

When Vernice Ferguson received the presidential chain in Indianapolis at the end of the biennial meeting in 1985, she named utilization of nursing research as the priority of the biennium. President Ferguson's 1986 message to the membership noted, "It is no small task to cull from the growing body of available research what will become known, accepted, and utilized in nursing practice" (1986, p.3). During her term as president, the regional assemblies emphasized the importance of building a culture supportive of nursing research. Ferguson was the keynote speaker at each of these assemblies during her term.

The Sigma Theta Tau International Presidential chain.

Sigma Theta Tau was renamed Sigma Theta Tau International at the 28th Biennial Convention in 1985.

To assist the society in achieving the goals of the 10-year plan, two members were added to the regional coordinating council. At the end of the 1985 biennium, there were seven regions in the Sigma Theta Tau network in the US.

Delegates to the 29th Biennial Convention in Indianapolis welcomed Angela Barron McBride to the presidency. It would be on her watch that the society would complete and dedicate the International Center for Nursing Scholarship.

Promoting Research and Scholarship

In 1983, a series of Research Notes, authored by members of the Research Committee, was presented in *Reflections*. These mini-tutorials could easily have found their way onto academic reading lists.

During the 1980s, *Reflections* became the vehicle through which the society promoted nursing research.

Since then, one issue of *Reflections* has been annually devoted to research. Jacqueline Fawcett, who headed the research committee in the early 1980s, compiled a comprehensive listing of the 102 recipients of Sigma Theta Tau's research fund awards for *Reflections*. Members were able to trace the role of the society in fostering research. For the first time, schools that offered postdoctoral training were also listed. The names and university affiliations of recently minted doctorally prepared nurses continued to be published in *Reflections*. Information about foundations interested in supporting nurse researchers and journals that published nursing research were also published. In 1983, the Calendar of Chapter Events was included, presenting a new face that focused on research symposia and programs around the globe. That same year, the *Directory of Nurse Researchers* was published, and a second edition followed in 1987.

In 1984, the governing council approved a Distinguished Lecturer Program. Rozella Schlotfeldt chaired the first selection committee. Participating lecturers were outstanding scholars who further advanced the dissemination of nursing science. In 1985, a day devoted to research opened each biennial meeting; this would become a tradition for all biennial meetings after 1985.

By 1985, *Reflections* had grown to 16 pages and was a full-color newsletter.

In 1987, Arista, a think tank on the nursing shortage, was hosted by Sigma Theta Tau International. The report of the think tank would be highlighted in 1988 when Distinguished Nurse Fellow Myrtle Aydelotte and Sigma Theta Tau International Treasurer Ron Norby presented testimony before the Bowen Commission on the nursing shortage. That same year, an international conference on health promotion at Wingspread was co-sponsored by Sigma Theta Tau International.

IN THIS ISSUE

Sigma Theta Tau International

REFLECTIONS

Volume 14, Number 1, Spring 1988

Charterings Reflect Growth, Vitality and International Development

IN THIS ISSUE

Sigma Theta Tau International

REFLECTIONS

Volume 15, Number 2, Summer 1995

Charterings Reflect Society's Rich Heritage

Although the fund-raising focus was on the new center, members continued to support research. As reported in 1986, 3,400 members and 200 chapters contributed to the research fund.

Sigma Theta Tau International

During the 1980s, Sigma Theta Tau International blossomed as an international organization. Madrid, Spain, was the site of a second international nursing congress in 1983. It was held in cooperation with the Universidad Complutense de Madrid School of Nursing. Attendees considered the dissemination and utilization of nursing research.

International outreach for Sigma Theta Tau continued during the ICN assemblies, with meetings and research conferences in Los Angeles, CA, in 1981 and in Israel in 1985. In Israel, ICN delegates elected a member of the society as an officer of ICN. In 1984, Sigma Theta Tau collaborated with the Korean Academic Nurses Society to present a research symposium addressing clinical scholarship. An international study program in Hong Kong; Taipei, Taiwan; and Seoul, Korea, was offered by Sigma Theta Tau after this research meeting. In 1987, Sigma Theta Tau International hosted a research congress in Edinburgh, Scotland, followed by an

international study tour. When ICN met in Seoul in 1989, the honor society cele-
brated the occasion by hosting a research conference in Taipei and installing new
international chapters-at-large at the National Taiwan University and National
Defense Medical Center in Taiwan, and at Yonsei University, Ewha Woman's
University, and Seoul National University in Korea. In 1987, Celebrate Worldwide
Nursing Scholarship was the theme of the 29th Biennial Convention in San
Francisco, CA.

In the mid 1980s, President Kelly focused on the international dimensions of the 10-year plan, highlighting the role of research. She also discussed international chapter development within the context of the three patterns that had emerged in the US: regular chapters, chapters-at-large, and alumni chapters. An honor society committee headed by Alice Redland offered four models for international conferences: the co-host model; the network model (use of international meetings to host research conferences); the scholarly outreach model (research programs are imported to the setting), and the multinational model (research conferences have multinational sponsorship and participants). These models guided the society's international programming well beyond the decade.

Sigma Theta Tau and the World of Philanthropy

The silent phase of the building drive ended in July 1979, when the national council officially announced the establishment of a building fund and invited members to join with those who had already contributed. In the 1980s, *Reflections* became Sigma Theta Tau's stewardship report. The names of donors to the building and research funds, along with recognition of memorial gifts, were published annually in *Reflections*. Chapters, as well as members, were encouraged to contribute to these funds. Special inserts in *Reflections* acknowledged member and chapter gifts. Although the fund-raising focus was on the new center, members continued to support research. In 1986, 3,400 members and 200 chapters contributed to the research fund.

Sigma Theta Tau had become serious about fund raising. In the spring 1980 *Reflections*, a reflective essay titled "Why a Building Fund?" (1980) was published. The author concluded that fund raising was necessary to provide services "which cultivate the development of nursing science and foster and nurture the nurse scholar" (p.2).

By 1986, Sigma Theta Tau International was poised to launch its first capital campaign. President Ferguson appointed two past presidents, Kelly and Sr. Donley, to chair the campaign. Kelly was named national chair and Sr. Donley was appointed member chair. Later Edgar B. Doris, vice president of the Corporate Affairs Division of Eli Lilly and Company, was named national corporate and foundations chair. President Ferguson, Kelly, and Sr. Donley hosted a satellite conference to launch the $4.6 million campaign. The conference reached 15 cities and 2,000 members. As reported in *Reflections*, the governing council focused on planning for the new center. To help provide funding for the center, the 1985 House of Delegates increased the annual renewal fee by $5. As part of its development effort, the first director of development, Linda Brimmer, was hired. *Reflections* was the voice of the capital campaign. Kelly (1987) reported on campaign progress in each issue, urging members and chapters to donate to the campaign. "With your help, we can build the Sigma Theta Tau Center for Nursing Scholarship. The plans cannot become reality without financial support from our Sigma Theta Tau International members" (p.6).

In the winter 1986 issue of *Reflections*, early investors in the campaign were presented in named circles and societies. The same issue revealed plans for the International Nursing Library, a state-of-the-art information resource center that would advance scholarship and research.

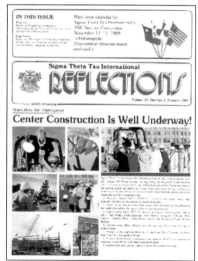

As development plans matured, the capital campaign was named the Knowledge Building Campaign. Members and corporate donors were invited to invest in the campaign by endowing pillars of knowledge in the International Nursing Library.

In January 1986, President Ferguson placed a bronze marker on the wall of Indiana University School of Nursing in recognition of its continued support of Sigma Theta Tau International since the society's founding in 1922. In 1987, the Board of Trustees of Indiana University provided land for the center on the northeast corner of the campus. The Sigma Theta Tau International Center for Nursing Scholarship would not be far from its original home.

The Center for Nursing Scholarship

The development of the Center for Nursing Scholarship dominated *Reflections* during the 1980s.

During her term as president, Lindeman urged Sigma Theta Tau members and all professional nurses to project an image of unity and strength. It was her hope that other nursing organizations would join Sigma Theta Tau in the Center for Nursing Scholarship. In late 1982, Watts announced that the Indianapolis community would fund a feasibility study for a Center for Nursing Scholarship that would be home to 25-30 nursing organizations. The governing council accepted the proposal. Unfortunately, the concept of unifying professional nursing in a Center for Nursing Scholarship did not find support in the nursing community. Sigma Theta Tau's governing council members went back to the drawing board.

In 1984, the Lilly Foundation awarded a planning grant to Sigma Theta Tau to study the development of a Center for Nursing Scholarship. Marjorie Beyers was named project director. As reported in the August-September 1985 issue of *Reflections*, Billye J. Brown and Glenn W. Irwin, vice president of Indiana University, were named co-chairs of the Project Advisory Committee.

Opened Doors

"It was one afternoon that no one there will ever forget" (Dedication, 1989a). The proud moment had arrived. The Sigma Theta Tau International Center for Nursing Scholarship was dedicated on Nov. 15, 1989.

"It was one afternoon that no one there will ever forget"

"November 15, 1989, was a stormy, gray and chilly day, but that didn't dampen enthusiasm" (Dedication, 1989b).

Mary Tolle Wright, the last of the founders, wrote on the occasion of the dedication: "I am as proud of Sigma Theta Tau International as I am of my two sons. Best wishes for the continued advancement of the society" (Dedication, 1989c). This dedication opened a new era for Sigma Theta Tau International and the development of nursing scholarship.

Sr. Rosemary Donley,

S R. ROSEMARY DONLEY has been an important leader and member of Sigma Theta Tau International for more than 4 decades. It was during her tenure as president that *Reflections*, the magazine known today as *Reflections on Nursing Leadership*, was created. She devoted much of her time and energy toward the early development of the honor society and was the only president to serve more than one term—actually serving 7 years as president. She provided leadership and instituted innovations during an important growth period. All of this combined made her the perfect person to write this important book that not only provides the reader with a history of the development of the honor society, but also mirrors many of the changes in nursing and healthcare.

Sr. Rosemary has continued to be involved in the activities of the honor society in a variety of ways, all while she has served in many important roles, including executive vice president at The Catholic University of America, as a nurse practitioner, and as a teacher.

Her interest in and devotion to Sigma Theta Tau International has been steady, even when managing her other substantial roles. We are privileged and proud to call her one of the honor society's treasures, and to say "thank you" to her for helping us understand our beloved nursing society better and for providing exemplary leadership over the years.

1975–1981

Carol Lindeman,
RN, PhD, FAAN

THANKS TO THE EFFORTS OF Sr. Rosemary Donley and Nell Watts, Sigma Theta Tau was ready to become a more vital force in nursing's leadership undertakings when I began my term as president in 1981. We needed a mobilizing force to move us into that position and to push us into becoming what we knew we could be. The hope was that a 10-year plan for the organization could be that mobilizing force. I thought that what held nursing together was its commitment to the health of the public. That premise became the core of the 10-year organizational plan for Sigma Theta Tau that was adopted as I became president and led us through the next several years.

We worked hard to create a center for nursing that could house all major nursing organizations. Unfortunately, although we had serious foundation funding, nursing organizations were unwilling to locate in Indianapolis, and that effort was dropped. However, the effort did facilitate the development of the current site for the honor society.

From a personal note, I thought the greatest part of Sigma Theta Tau was the way people related to each other. We always left a meeting feeling better than when we arrived. How many others can say that?

Lucie Kelly,
RN, PhD, FAAN

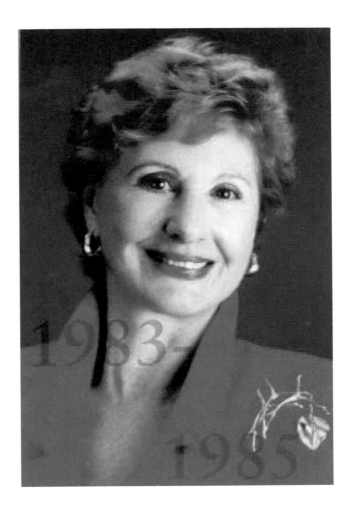

LOOKING BACK ON MY TERM as president from 1983 to 1985, the three things I thought were most important were starting the formal process of building the international aspects of Sigma Theta Tau, launching a mentoring award—something that was very close to my heart—and signing the land lease and beginning preparations for building the Center for Nursing Scholarship.

Our international efforts were centered not only on our presence at international conferences, but also on our grass-roots efforts in meeting and educating every nurse we could about the values, vision, and mission of the society. It was literally a nurse-to-nurse effort to connect ourselves internationally with other nurses and nursing organizations. Without a doubt, it was great fun to personally meet with nurses from all around the world and from all walks of life. I treasure those memories.

I'm equally proud of our work in preparing for the headquarters building in Indianapolis. What an interesting and important process that was!

I'm equally as proud—for different reasons—of the mentoring award, because mentoring was very important in my career and my life. To have the award named after me and to become the second recipient and be recognized as Sr. Rosemary Donley's mentor were great personal honors.

Reflections now is very different from *Reflections* when I was president, but in many ways it's exactly the same. What's most important and most lasting is the purpose of *Reflections*—to bring the membership together as a community. What it did then and still does is to reach nurses at all levels and make them more knowledgeable about nursing.

Vernice D. Ferguson,
RN, MA, FAAN

I BECAME PRESIDENT AT an exciting time. It was in Lucie Kelly's term as president—which immediately preceded mine—that Sigma Theta Tau moved into the international arena. This international momentum continued to build during my term in office from 1985 to 1987. In addition, I focused much energy and attention on propelling the efforts forward for a head-quarters building in Indianapolis, IN, with the funds required. I spent considerable time on cultivation visits in Indianapolis and beyond in the larger community. Glenn Irwin, who had retired in 1986 as chancellor of Indiana University-Purdue University Indianapolis, was "court-ed" and accepted the chair of the major fund-raising campaign. Our magnificent building is testimony in part to the success of these efforts.

Reflections has always been a voice of relevance for Sigma Theta Tau International. It remains so today as it continues to grow and change befitting the society's ever expanding influence.

1985–

1987

Angela Barron McBride,
RN, PhD, FAAN

I WAS PRESIDENT OF Sigma Theta Tau International when the society chartered the first chapters beyond the US (Canada, Korea, Taiwan) and during the building of our headquarters. These experiences taught me a great deal about leadership. Some of the critical things I learned were:

- **Networking is vitally important.** Because I had a history of professional involvement, I had many colleagues around the US and beyond. I learned one should never underestimate the networking power of these linkages, for it meant I was able to engage a cross-section of talent in the work of the society during my term in office.

- **You will be successful in office if you build on your strengths.** Because I was a wife and mother, I knew firsthand about juggling work and family issues. Because so many society members were doing the same juggling, I focused all of the regional assembles on such matters, with record attendance.

- **If the leader stays on message, then others will hear the message.** The themes of the biennium were importantly reinforced through the pages of *Reflections* and other Sigma Theta Tau International publications.

- **Fund raising is a leadership skill.** During the 1987-89 biennium, we obtained a site for the headquarters building, completed the architectural design, raised more than half of the monies needed for the project, and dedicated the new building. This experience convinced me that philanthropy is not about asking for money, but about helping professionals to collectively achieve their dreams.

- **Being involved internationally helps you understand your home situation better.** When we chartered the first chapters outside the US, I had an opportunity to work intimately with colleagues elsewhere and to see practices that made me rethink how we were doing things locally. I realized that "going international" was less about outreach and more about getting out of your comfort zone so you can rethink your own assumptions.

Thanks to the leadership opportunities provided me as Sigma Theta Tau International president, I learned a great deal about working in complex systems, and that experience has served me well.

Billye J. Brown,

RN, EdD, FAAN

ONE OF THE THINGS THAT always impressed me about the honor society, from even my earliest professional days, is that we set the standard for professional organizations. Many people and many other organizations look to us as a model. That's something to be proud of!

My term of office as president from 1989 to 1991 gave me two of the best years of my life as far as my own involvement with other nurse leaders, the organization, and with members. Interestingly, I often tell people that I would have been a better dean if I had been named dean after being president of the honor society! I learned so much and had the chance to be closely involved with the business side, with the fund-raising side, and with the analysis and planning for significant changes. It was an extremely important learning opportunity in my life and an important period of change facilitation for the organization.

When reflecting back on all we were able to do during my term, I think of three significant accomplishments. One of the first was reinvesting 10% of the interest for all interest-bearing endowment funds to extend and sustain the funds. We also named the Virginia Henderson International Nursing Library and worked hard on establishing online accessibility. In terms of scope of changes, the appointment of a blue-ribbon task force to analyze the organizational structure was enormous. Among outcomes from their assessment was the recommendation to change the governing council to the board of directors. This was a crucial change that gave the executive team and staff the room to conduct the business of running the organization.

What I found is that what occurred didn't happen so much because of me, but because of a stage of readiness that was brought about by my predecessors and by the hard work of Nell Watts and everyone at the honor society. The accomplishments of any president are the accomplishments of a smart team of hard-working, creative, and courageous people.

What does all this have to do with *Reflections on Nursing Leadership* (*RNL*), you might ask? The simple answer is "communication." Without communication to and with members, very little of what we do could be accomplished. *RNL* was my means of communicating with members. Just imagine all the information that went out when we were going to vote on changing the governing council. The key to that was getting as much information as possible out there. *RNL* allowed us to do that effectively and efficiently. I think that's why it went so smoothly when we went to the House of Delegates. It's been an important voice for all of us, and now with the new *RNL* online, I see communication being so much quicker, easier, and current. I look forward to seeing more award-winning *RNL* issues in years to come.

Beth Vaughan-Wrobel,
RN, EdD, FAAN

M Y PRESIDENTIAL TERM, 1991-1993, coincided with a time of great change for the organization. In addition to focusing on The Leadership Challenge in Nursing and the many firsts that went along with attaining our goals for the biennium, I experienced many firsts and lasts in my unusual position as a transitional leader. My short list of leadership-based team successes during my term includes:

- Establishing a leadership intern program, with an intern from each of the seven regions supported in learning about organizational leadership and a leadership project of her or his choosing.

- Establishing a leadership extern project at the chapter level with the same goals as the internship program.

- Offering the first Nell J. Watts Lifetime Achievement Award, recognizing excellence in leadership.

- Offering the first Audrey Hepburn Award for excellence in pediatric nursing.

- Implementing the International Leadership Institute.

- Establishing *The Online Journal of Knowledge Synthesis for Nursing.*

- Presenting the first technology day, held the day before convention, to focus on technology in nursing leadership.

- Initiating formal orientation for chapter installation. A professional videotape about the installation process was made available to all chapters.

As I mentioned, it was a time of great transition, and I oversaw the last governing council as we made plans and worked to evolve this governing body to a board of directors. In addition, I was the last president to work with Nell J. Watts. After 20 years as executive officer, she transitioned her leadership to the capable hands of Nancy Dickenson-Hazard. It was indeed the ending of one era and the beginning of a whole new era that would see Sigma Theta Tau International rise to even greater heights as the pre-eminent nursing organization.

1991–

1993

1993–
1995

Fay L. Bower,
RN, DNSc, FAAN

DURING MY TENURE AS president of Sigma Theta Tau International, from 1993 to 1995, I continued the focus on leadership initiated by the previous president, Beth Vaughan-Wrobel. The Leadership Institute, which I helped develop as president-elect, was expanded, as was the mentor program. It was clear to me and others that we needed more leadership preparation for nurses and that our members were excellent candidates for leadership roles. Looking to the future, the board and I saw the need for more programs that would help nurses develop leadership skills, as there was a need for more nurse influence in the management of patient care. *Reflections* was one of the major ways of getting this message out to members and to nurses around the world. Within the pages of *Reflections,* we highlighted leadership programs and told stories of nurses who had been mentored.

The Arista conferences were also expanded during my presidency. Without *Reflections,* we would not have been able to get the message out to those around the globe. We were growing with the establishment of chapters throughout the world, and keeping members aware of the impact of that growth was not an easy task. We were learning daily how to function as an international organization; with the help of articles in *Reflections,* that message was conveyed to all members.

The Arista conferences were a first for the society and were very important, as they brought leaders from around the world together at various places around the globe. While we did not all speak the same language, we did have similar concerns about nursing and healthcare. The dialogue was very valuable, and it helped us reinforce our values related to leadership, scholarship, and research.

I will never forget those two years of my presidency, as I had the privilege of serving a large constituency during a time of growth and change. It was a challenge and a thrill to see successful programs initiated and to be part of the installation of new chapters throughout the world. I learned a lot about nursing in other countries and about the need for strong leadership in nursing in many areas of the globe. A review of many articles in *Reflections* during that time and to the present can bring anyone to see the many changes that have occurred over time in nursing throughout the world.

From a small, four-page newsletter, *Reflections* has become an important chronicle of the change experienced by members like me. I am proud of my tenure as president and of my membership in an organization that has made such a major impact on the discipline of nursing. Scholarship, research, and leadership are still important aspects of nursing and are still reported in *Reflections* as major components of nursing in this changing world of healthcare.

Melanie Dreher,

RN, PhD, FAAN

MY TERM FROM 1995 TO 1997 was a very special, exciting time because it was the 75th anniversary of Sigma Theta Tau International. The celebration was spectacular, and *Reflections* really showed that.

My term was one of the few in which leadership was not the central focus; our focus was on clinical scholarship. It was quite different from those that preceded it and those that followed. For me, it was a very exciting and vibrant time. It was quite special because we were finally admitting that a nurse didn't have to be a faculty member to be a scholar.

So many of our members are clinicians, and I think what we did in terms of clinical scholarship—with the clinical scholar document and the focus on the clinical scholar—helped to lay the groundwork, the foundation, for the clinical scholarship work that is sweeping the nursing community.

Writing the *Reflections* editorials was important. I remember well writing those editorials! I agonized over them and I procrastinated writing them, but then when I sat down and wrote them, I became inspired … genuinely inspired. I was so touched by the people I was writing for. Remarkably, I have had people thank me for those editorials! If I inspired them even a small degree compared to how they inspired me, I will be appreciative and thankful, too, for the role *Reflections* played in my ability to reach out with my message.

1995–1997

Eleanor Sullivan,
RN, PhD, FAAN

THE YEARS BETWEEN 1997 AND 1999 were exciting, challenging, and demanding, as we were charged with developing the strategic plan for the start of the new millennium. Using the theme Avenues to the Future, a strategic planning task force and more than 1,000 members worldwide who participated in "dream teams" created "Strategic Plan 2005," which concludes this year. I was honored and humbled to lead the Honor Society of Nursing, Sigma Theta Tau International during such productive years.

Reflections gave me an opportunity each quarter to share my ideas and experiences with readers as we planned for the future. This was essential to being inclusive in our efforts and contributed to the overwhelming response from members (more than 1000) as they submitted their ideas to the strategic planning team.

1997–1999

Pat Thompson, RN, EdD, FAAN

1999–2001

URING MY TERM IN OFFICE from 1999 to 2001, I was fortunate to be involved with the program sponsored by the American International Health Alliance (AIHA) and Sigma Theta Tau Inter-national that focused on leadership, scholarship, and policy development of nurses from the New Independent States of the former Soviet Union and Central and Eastern Europe. Nurses completing this program applied these skills in their home countries and made positive health care changes. To be able to teach these nurses ... to be able to watch as they prepared to take what we had shown them and profoundly change the lives of so many in their communities—at the most basic levels in some cases—was a privilege and a lasting honor. What's more, we had the chance to meet and work with physician deans and directors of nursing programs in these regions to define strategies for incorporating nursing scholarship and leadership into their programs.

I also had the privilege to be part of the October 2000 International Academic Nursing Alliance (IANA) at the Carter Center in Atlanta, GA, when representatives from 28 countries established an advisory committee and 10 work groups for the alliance. Imagine people from 28 countries coming together and working with the same goal in mind! It was quite amazing, because everyone was there with one mind and one goal and worked together so well for the common good.

This brings me to *Reflections on Nursing Leadership (RNL)* and its focus on serving the membership. We've been fortunate that *RNL* has grown along with the honor society. It has changed and evolved with the membership, and it has become an excellent way to distribute information about leadership to the membership. I viewed my quarterly letters as an opportunity to speak directly to members to keep them updated on honor society news and progress. It was amazing to me that I would hear back from many in relation to my messages or to what the organization was doing. It was refreshing to speak directly to them and get to know them. *RNL* is also a way for members to know us as people, as leaders, and as presidents, both personally and professionally. It has also become a way for nurses around the world to share stories in those pages. Through profiles and stories, *RNL* has helped drive home the message that leadership does not reside exclusively in people with high-level titles. In the pages of *RNL*, you see nurses, no matter what their position, engaged day-to-day in leading others. These nurses are sometimes in difficult and trying circumstances. Time and again, we are shown that the honor society has outstanding members who are out there demonstrating leadership and our core values.

May L. Wykle,
RN, PhD, FAAN

ONE OF THE MOST exciting highlights of my nursing career was serving as president of Sigma Theta Tau International from 2001 to 2003. I have always loved the work of the honor society and was proud to be elected a member of Alpha Mu Chapter. To have the opportunity to gain firsthand knowledge of the organization as president and to work with Chief Executive Officer Nancy Dickenson-Hazard, the headquarters staff, and the outstanding board of directors were wonderful learning experiences. I found the operation of the organization to be "top shelf" in its mission and vision for better healthcare through nursing and its goal to contribute to the improvement of global health. It is truly an organization that elevates the quality of nursing education and the quest for better patient outcomes based on evidence.

I continue to be very impressed with the honor society's publications and their international focus on research. The organization's strong efforts to support the professional nurse through continuing education and career development are remarkable. As a benefit of membership, all active members receive the honor society's research journal, *Journal of Nursing Scholarship (JNS)*, as well as the quarterly member newsmagazine, *Reflections on Nursing Leadership (RNL)*. *JNS* provides members with ongoing access to cutting-edge nursing research and clinical applications, while *RNL* documents the many wonderful accomplishments that honor society members and other nurses are making throughout the world.

2001–
2003

Daniel J. Pesut,
PhD, APRN, BC, FAAN

As president of the Honor Society of Nursing, Sigma Theta Tau International from 2003 to 2005, I enjoyed communicating with the membership via the "Message From the President" feature. I valued and appreciated the editorial planning, creative thought, and foresight devoted to the quarterly features. For example, as I was preparing my Presidential Call to Action: Create the Future Through Renewal, Jim Mattson, *Reflections on Nursing Leadership (RNL)* editor, was working toward the development of themes that would complement the call and reinforce the message.

The eight issues associated with my term in office tapped the following themes: renewal through attention to self; reflective practice; reinventing the workplace; finding purpose through service; shaping government and organizational policy; weighing the evidence of nursing science; doing what's right: the ethics of nursing; and consideration of the preferred future of nursing.

What was rewarding and meaningful to me was Jim's openness to suggestions about potential authors and stories. As I traveled and represented the honor society, I would admire and appreciate projects or works that engaged people's efforts. I frequently encouraged people to contact Jim or visit the honor society home page and click on the publications page to learn more about submitting a story for *RNL*. When I returned home, I would often follow up with an e-mail and connect Jim with the people who were "living the stories." Jim faithfully followed up and worked with people to make their contributions. Members I met during my presidential journeys contributed many of the stories featured in the 2003-2005 editions of *RNL*.

As the newsmagazine moves to an online format, I suspect some people will miss sitting down and fingering their way through the stories. However, I am excited about the possibilities and potentials associated with stories and features that enable people to visit supplemental Web links and additional resources. With a click of the mouse, members can explore, connect, and learn more through the nursing leadership stories that are shared and circulated. The online version of *RNL* is another portal for accessing the international nursing knowledge network and building a global community of nurse leaders.

2003–

2005

More comprehensive than a newsletter and less formal than a scholarly journal, *Reflections* was designed to raise the profile of nurses as scholars and to present their engagement in healthcare decision making within the scientific community.

Reflecting Forward: 1990–1999

B Y THE ADVENT OF the 1990s, Sigma Theta Tau International had grown to nearly 300 chapters with almost 100,000 members. Those in the US nursing world had fought hard for the right to establish the National Center for Nursing Research (NCNR) and were closing in on the 1993 victory that would make the NCNR into a separate institute within the National Institutes of Health, where it would be renamed the National Institute for Nursing Research (NINR). The advanced practice nurse movement was gaining strength and steam as more and more nurses were furthering their educations, their careers, and their practices. Both charitable organizations and governments had begun to focus monies and energies on the cyclic nursing shortages, hoping to solve them before the unprecedented and looming shortages that were forecast for the 2000s and after. Nursing organizations around the globe were stronger and more politically astute than ever before, and they were working together for common goals like never before.

All in all, the 1990s brought significant opportunities for Sigma Theta Tau International to set the standards for nursing scholarship, research, and technological advancements.

Epitomizing the decade of the 1990s for the society, the 33rd Biennial Convention in Detroit, MI, in 1995 was characterized in *Reflections* as a Hallmark of Merit. The 1,900 participants paid special tribute and honored distinguished members with the following newly created awards:

- Nell J. Watts Lifetime Achievement in Nursing Award

- Lucie S. Kelly Mentor Award

- Public Service Award

- Audrey Hepburn Award for Contributions to the Health and Welfare of Children

- Episteme Award

- Dorothy Ford Buschmann Presidential Award

In the spring of 1995, Executive Officer Nancy Dickenson-Hazard compared the society of 1922 to the society of 1995. A few of the statistics she provided stand out in particular:

1995 Biennial Convention of the Honor Society of Nursing, Sigma Theta Tau International.

Looking back at the legacy of the past in the spring 1995 *Reflections.*

■ The society had grown from six members (the founders) in 1922 to 200,000 in 1995.

■ The society had grown from one chapter in Indiana in 1922 to 346 chapters worldwide in 1995.

■ The society had grown from one research grant in 1922 to 232 grants in 1995.

On the 20th anniversary of the founding of *Reflections,* Sr. Rosemary Donley described the magazine as a communication vehicle to challenge, encourage, and recognize members and as a mode for listening and speaking. More comprehensive than a newsletter and less formal than a scholarly journal, *Reflections* was designed to raise the profile of nurses as scholars and to present their engagement in healthcare decision making within the scientific community.

Five different presidents who served the society in the 1990s—Billye Brown, Beth Vaughan-Wrobel, Fay Bower, Melanie Dreher, and Eleanor Sullivan—and their leadership activities were described in *Reflections* throughout the decade. In addition, obituaries were posted and deaths were mourned as two of the original founders of Sigma Theta Tau—Elizabeth McWilliams Miller on Nov. 25, 1993, and Mary Tolle Wright on Feb. 20, 1999—were lost and their lives remembered in the pages of *Reflections.* Virginia Henderson, a woman who embodied the spirit of the society, died at age 98 on March 19, 1995. A Festschrift honoring Virginia Henderson, *Signature for Nursing,* edited by Eleanor Krohn Herrmann, was made available by the society.

Honoring Virginia Henderson.

Virginia Henderson, seated on the right, signs her consent to allow Sigma Theta Tau International to endow the library in the Center for Nursing Scholarship in her name, to be called the Virginia Henderson International Nursing Library. Billye Brown is seated to her right. In the back, from left, are Linda A. Lewandowski, Judith B. Krauss, James A. Fain, and Nell Watts.

Billye Brown envisioned the Action for the 1990s agenda as a continuing commitment to the development, dissemination, and utilization of knowledge. She worked to create a structure for the society that would facilitate its growth and mission. As the decade began, the society boasted 158,000 members and planned to charter 38 chapters in the first biennium of the decade. Further changes were brewing, as executive leadership and President Brown appointed a blue-ribbon task force to assess the organizational structure of the society and make recommendations for change. Among the more significant outcomes from this group was the recommendation to remake the governing council into a board of directors, effectively enlarging the board and placing policy, planning, and resource development for the international organization within the board's purview. Having *Reflections* as a communication tool was instrumental in publicizing the reorganization recommendations that would eventually be passed by the House of Delegates at the 1991 convention.

Billye Brown, 18th president of Sigma Theta Tau International, is widely recognized as the mother of Sigma Theta Tau International fund raising.

Beth Vaughan-Wrobel inaugurated her presidency at the end of the 1991 Biennial Convention in Tampa, FL, with a renewed emphasis on nursing leadership. During her tenure, the International Leadership Institute was created. Subsuming all leadership activities, the institute encompassed the leadership intern and extern programs, the second Arista conference, a scholar-in-residence program with a focus on leadership, a "Leadership Profile Series" in *Reflections,* and the designation of a theme for the 1991-93 regional assemblies—Building for the Future Through Nursing Leadership.

Beth Vaughan-Wrobel, 19th president of Sigma Theta Tau. 1991-1993.

President Fay Bower embraced research utilization, promoting the relevance and value of clinical nursing research as a framework for practice. Leadership and development of members also placed high on Bower's agenda. Many of the leadership initiatives were promoted, and chapter involvement in those programs was encouraged. Influenced by her study of servant leadership, Bower was actively engaged in strengthening the leadership potential of individual members.

Fay L. Bower, 20th president of Sigma Theta Tau International. 1993-1995.

Nurse anthropologist Melanie Dreher emphasized clinical scholarship and cultural diversity during her presidency, identifying cross-cultural concepts that were important for nursing research: women's health, clinical decision making, nursing technology, comfort, suffering and pain management, and incontinence. During her tenure, the Scholar-in-Residence Exchange Program was established. Like her predecessors, Dreher promoted translation and dissemination of research using the regional assemblies to advance clinical scholarship.

Melanie C. Dreher, 21st president of Sigma Theta Tau International. 1995-1997

Eleanor Sullivan became the 22nd president of Sigma Theta Tau International at the close of the 75th anniversary celebration. In her charge to the House of Delegates, she addressed Avenues to the Future and pledged to:

- Strengthen the global diversity of Sigma Theta Tau International

- Envision a preferred future for the next millennium

- Engage in strategic alliances with collaborative partners

- Showcase nursing and nursing research as cornerstones to global healthcare delivery

Eleanor Sullivan, 22nd president of Sigma Theta Tau International. 1997-1999.

Eleanor Sullivan's presidential charge in the first quarter 1998 issue of *Reflections*.

The summer 1992 issue of *Reflections* announced the resignation of Nell J. Watts as executive officer. Watts' legacy was chronicled in the fall 1993 issue of *Reflections*. Past President Billye Brown and current President Beth Vaughan-Wrobel credited the commitment and caring of Watts for the growth in Sigma Theta Tau International; Vernice Ferguson described Watts as a legend; President-Elect Fay Bower called her a visionary; Lucie Kelly said she was a risk taker; Angela Barron McBride cited her generous spirit; and Sr. Rosemary Donley expressed awe in her ability to manage complexity. Watts' memoir, *The Adventuresome Years: Leaders in Action 1973 to 1993*, was published in 1997 by the honor society to celebrate the 75th anniversary.

Nell Watts, executive officer of Sigma Theta Tau since 1974, celebrated her retirement in 1993.

SIGMA THETA TAU INTERNATIONAL

REFLECTIONS

Translating The Vision Into Reality

In 75 years, the Honor Society of Nursing, Sigma Theta Tau International had:

- Inducted around 250,000 members;
- Installed 356 chapters.

Sigma Theta Tau International demographics in 1997

- 120,000 active members in ...
- 70 countries and territories.
- Sixty-two percent held master's degrees,
- 69% worked full time,
- 50% were employed in hospitals, and
- 26% were staff nurses.

LEADERSHIP PROFILE

A Tribute To Nell J. Watts

By LUCIE S. KELLY, RN, PhD, FAAN

In January 1974, Nell J. Watts, who had been the Executive Director of the Indiana League for Nursing, took the position of Executive Officer at Sigma Theta Tau International and for Nell Watts. At the organization's 50th anniversary celebration at the 22nd biennial convention the previous fall, President Ruth Stepfer and Vice President Sister Rosemary Donley got the support of the membership to initiate this new position for Sigma Theta Tau clearly needed an officer and some professional management. Preliminary contact had been made with Emily Holmquist, then Dean of the Indiana University (IU) School of Nursing, about the possibility of space, and she was agreeable, as was her successor, Dr. Elizabeth Grossman and the administration of IU; therefore, by the end of 1974, the nursing honor society that had begun at IU was once more part of the family, with two offices, one part-time secretary, and Nell Watts.

"Sigma Theta Tau has become the great organization that it is today because of the commitment and caring of Nell Watts for our international organization, chapters and members. When a new initiative is being considered Nell always asks 'How will this benefit the members of Sigma Theta Tau?'"

— Dr. Beth C. Vaughan Wrobel
President 1991 - 1993

Rebecca (Becky) Markel, faculty IU SON, who was an active participant at these new beginnings and who remains a stalwart worker and supporter, was asked why Nell would leave an established position

Nell J. Watts, Executive Officer
(1974-1993)

"Nell Watts is a legend in her lifetime. All of us at Sigma Theta Tau, leaders and followers, are grateful for the pivotal role she has played through the years. In large measure because of her, we proudly proclaim the growth and vibrancy of an unparalleled international honor society for nursing."

— Dr. Vernice Ferguson,
President 1975 - 1981

Development Committee, Becky and consultant Lee Cotton they created the "Avenues for Action" concept that gave members opportunities to have an impact on the development of nursing scholarship. For the first time, Sigma Theta Tau had as exhibit at the National League for Nursing in 1974 and the American Nurses Association in 1976, which reintroduced the honor society to nurses. Nell only raised the idea of chapter-at-large to provide visibility to potential chapters that could not survive in one school.

Dynamic programs were introduced over the years, with chapters at active participants in various regions where they

were held. With energetic committees they encompassed writing and publishing nursing theories, nursing research, grant writing, and eventually, the popular regional conferences that combined scholarly presentations by nursing leaders with a day of chapter development. Nell not only helped to plan and produce these programs, but also participated. Even more exciting was the initiation of the international research conferences in Spain, Israel, Korea, Taiwan, and Scotland in cooperation with universities in those countries. The papers presented by nurses from around the world were impressive.

Although Nell was, and is, the first to give credit to the members and officers who came up with ideas and suggested speakers for all the programs, the burden

---

Nell J. Watts and Beth Vaughan Wrobel (President) in the Texas Room at the International Center for Nursing Scholarship.

"Although our founders established an organization that was destined to grow and develop, one wonders whether, if it would have been international and grown to its present size and influence without the guidance of Nell Watts. I think not, and I'm grateful for her twenty years of progressive leadership of the society."

— Dr. Billye J. Brown
President 1989 - 1991

fashion, to answer the endless queries, to resolve endless problems, to raise the needed funds, and to support and encourage the members of the grassroots clearly was passed on Nell Watts and the responsibilities was in good hands. She was the executive who, over the years, had set up headquarters in a business-like mode, had developed the necessary policies and procedures, had straightened the records, had employed and supervised the increasing staff as Sigma Theta Tau grew. But most of all she was the heart of Sigma Theta Tau: the professional who was available to advise as chapters also grew and as new

"Nell Watts has a vision: She sees a big picture while she holds a myriad of details in her hands. She has an incredible respect for the members of Sigma Theta Tau. The members have been the source of her inspiration and the font of her energy as she has built Sigma Theta Tau into an international organization of scholars."

— Sister Rosemary Donley
President 1975 - 1981

ones were chartered (a 600% growth overall) members turned to "Nell," as they inevitably called her, for help and they got it. Chapter officers have continually contacted repeatedly with some astonishment, that they were never brushed off, treated impersonally, or made to call back to an endless number of people as happens so often in organizations. They needed questions answered; they got questions answered with patience, courtesy, and real concern. If they needed Nell personally, that's who answered, but most important of all, the time she set, that staff were available to support members, was demonstrated daily. Nell believed in an informed membership, and she was skilled in pulling together the odds and ends of information into coherent policies. And her extraordinary commitment to Sigma Theta Tau was demonstrated daily.

Over the years and under Nell's leadership, Sigma Theta Tau had many

firsts in which Nell was a major actor: increased research awards and research programs, developed a series of historical and other educational videotapes, updated annually a list of the doctoral graduates and programs, initiated *Reflections* which became more than a newsletter, enabled *IMAGE* to become recognized as a valuable scholarly nursing journal, published the *Directory of Nurse Researchers* which is also available on computer, established a development program that resulted in a

---

LEADERSHIP PROFILE

magnificent building, implemented the vision of an international electronic library, and earned ongoing recognition and support from members, corporations and foundations.

But, Nell Watts will say, "only with the commitment, imagination, and hard work of officers and members in their many roles." Yes, Nell, of course, but equally with your support, your ideas, and your communication of the concepts into reality. Working with members in a collegial team nothing was impossible. It took courage for the officers and Nell to make Sigma Theta Tau an international organization, and it was Nell who worked on the logistics. It took even more courage to take the steps that committed the organization to a capital campaign. It took skill and good judgment to prepare the initial studies and to select an outstanding director of development and together arrange for the additional studies, and initiate contacts with funding

"Not only has Nell Watts accomplished much herself, but she has the conceptual ability and generosity of spirit to describe the principles that she has applied in order to benefit others."

— Dr. Angela Barron McBride,
President 1987 - 1989

prospects. Because of the respect in which Nell was held in the Indianapolis community, doors were opened. She had many professional and business colleagues upon whom she could draw for advice, many of whom were important community leaders. (They were also willing to share their know-how with board members and committee chairs in think sessions that gave us all a little different perspective on how to attack an issue or move in other directions.)

Shown above
Sigma Theta Tau Gala Banquet honoring Audrey Hepburn in the Indiana Roof Ballroom, Indianapolis, in April 1992.

Shown at left
Groundbreaking for the new International Center for Nursing Scholarship, 1989

Nell received many honors in Indianapolis: Indiana Nurse of the Year Award presented by the Illinois Foundation and the Indiana League for Nursing, a citation by the Indiana University-Purdue University for her "leadership vision and commitment to professional nursing and significant contributions to our mutual development." Distinguished Alumni award from I. U. School of Nursing.

Of course, a cap to her accomplishments was the honorary doctor of science degree awarded in I U in 1990. And on a national level her election into the American Academy of Nursing was a special recognition by her peers. Within Sigma Theta Tau, there are also many indications of the members' regard for her: Chapters and individual members donation of funds toward the $35,000 pillar in the Center for Nursing Scholarship and more recently, as one more acknowledgment of her own leadership, the initiation of a fund for the Nell J. Watts Leadership Institute.

"I've never heard Nell say, 'That's impossible, too difficult, unreasonable' only 'we'll work it out.' She's a risk-taker in the best sense of the phrase."

— Dr. Lucie Kelly,
President 1983 - 1985

As Nell retires from the position of executive officer, it is only one more element of her relationship to Sigma Theta Tau and her professional career. She will continue to be supportive and helpful in development and other activities, as requested. She is already in demand by other groups as a consultant and to help plan conferences. She may even have a little more time for her husband, Leslie Ewbo should by now be an honorary Sigma Theta Tau member, and daughters, Cynthia (Cindy), an attorney in Los Angeles, and Anita, a computer expert in Washington, D.C. and always will that be a very special Sigma Theta Tau member and stay in the hearts of all her colleagues ∎

Nancy Dickenson-Hazard, the new executive officer for the society, was featured on the cover of *Reflections* in the spring of 1994.

Nancy Dickenson-Hazard, then, as featured in the spring 1994 issue of *Reflections* ...
... And now in her most recent *Reflections on Nursing Leadership* "Notes from the Chief Executive Officer" in the third quarter 2005 issue.

Dickenson-Hazard observed that over its 75-year history, the society had inducted around 250,000 members and installed 356 chapters. At the beginning of 1997, Sigma Theta Tau International had 120,000 active members in 70 countries and territories. Sixty-two percent of those members held master's degrees; 69% worked full time; 50% were employed in hospitals; and 26% were staff nurses.

To celebrate the 75th anniversary, the society commissioned a video called "The Company We Keep." The 34th Biennial Convention and the celebration of the 75th anniversary were nicely described in *Reflections* in the first quarter issue of 1998. The advancement of nursing and the various forces within and without the profession in each decade were also chronicled in *Reflections*.

Working for the Future of Nursing

In the spring of 1990, Billye Brown reflected on the Sigma Theta Tau International 10-year plan, A Blueprint of Excellence, and noted the accomplishments of the 1980s:

- Significant increases in chapter support for research;

- Development of the International Center for Nursing Scholarship;

- Development of the Virginia Henderson International Nursing Library;

- Creation of a development department;

- Chapters located in every state in the US and in Canada, Taiwan, and Korea;

- Research utilization increased; and

- International research congresses co-sponsored in Spain, Korea, Israel, Scotland, and Taiwan.

Watts presented a primer on convention management with an account on the planning, implementation, and evaluation of the 31st Biennial Convention in *Reflections*.

Further, the history of *Image, the Journal of Nursing Scholarship* was described as seen through the eyes of its past editors—Beatrice Goodwin, Frances Cleary, Mary Magula, Lucie Young Kelly, Sr. Rosemary Donley, and Donna Diers—on the occasion of the journal's 25th anniversary. Beverly Henry became the new editor of *Image, the Journal of Nursing Scholarship* in July 1993. She was succeeded by Sue Thomas Hegyvary in 1999.

In late 1993, a new *Reflections* series called "Profiles of Nursing Leaders" was created. The summer 1993 issue featured Vernice Ferguson, scholar-at-large. "During her term as president of Sigma Theta Tau International, from 1985-87, she worked fervently to encourage members to utilize the findings of research in their practice" (Fondiller, 1993, p. 5).

In 1996, 26 experts invited to participate in Arista II met under the banner "Healthy People Leaders in Partnership." Chaired by Fay Bower and supported by a grant from the W.K. Kellogg Foundation, Arista II's interdisciplinary participants examined the restructuring of healthcare services, defining five areas of importance: public communication, policy making, education, leadership development, research models, and partnerships. Arista II participants recommended immediate and long-term strategies for action.

Now completed, the Arista series, an initiative of the Honor Society of Nursing, Sigma Theta Tau International, was designed to bring the best thinking to bear in confronting health issues of global significance, providing a multinational interdisciplinary platform from which to influence the change of nursing practice.

The Arista think-tank meetings, named for the Greek word meaning "the brightest," assembled experts and reactors to converse, debate, find consensus, and develop strategies for the future of nursing in an era of continuing health sector reform.

In 1997, the society participated with the University of Rochester School of Nursing in a study of how nurses are portrayed in the media. The findings of the Woodhull Media Project were presented at the 34th Biennial Convention in December 1997. The report noted that although a patient quickly realizes how important nurses are, the media continue to ignore their role.

The Woodhull Media Project studied how nurses were portrayed in the media.

In 1999, the *HeART of Nursing* (a book of nurses' artworks) was announced in *Reflections,* with a call for contributions that invited members to share examples of their expressive and creative artworks. Selected submissions were showcased at the 1999 Biennial Convention in San Diego, CA, US.

The Distinguished Lecturer Program celebrated its 10th anniversary in 1997 and boasted 118 distinguished lecturers.

At the end of the 1990s, *Reflections* offered glimpses into the world of nurse entrepreneurs. Creativity and diversity described the businesses of members Ann Van Slyck, Kathleen Vollman, Marie Manthey, and Melodie Chenevert.

Van Slyck's multimillion-dollar company manages patient and staff information and financial data for healthcare facilities. She described four main responsibilities of a consultant entrepreneur: to deliver the service, to manage the business, to become increasingly expert in the product, and to develop a full appreciation for marketing and sales. Inventor Kathleen Vollman described how she developed and tested the Vollman Prone Positioner, a device to position patients with severe respiratory distress. Marie Manthey, who began a consulting company that assists acute-care and long-term care facilities, is associated with primary

Humorist and designer Melodie Chenevert is one of the entrepreneurial nurse leaders profiled in Reflections.

Research by Lois Evans and Neville Strumpf concerning use of restraints in caring for older patients was reported in the third quarter 1996 issue of *Reflections*. Not long after this article was published, institutions and governmental agencies began changing their policies on restraints in elder care.

nursing—which she calls a grass-roots miracle. Melodie Chenevert, humorist and designer, described her portable career. She transformed her books into speaking engagements and founded Pro-Nurse, a company that sells products and services that cultivate professional pride.

Promoting Nursing Research and Scholarship

The third quarter 1996 issue of *Reflections* presented evidence that nursing practice had a scientific base. The lead article featured the research of Lois Evans and Neville Strumpf, who compared individualized care to the use of restraints in hospitals and nursing homes. Other research-based studies covered in *Reflections* included the impact of high-tech environments on premature infants; the effect of cognitive, behavioral therapy on the recurrence of heart attacks and death; the relationship of physical activity and exercise to heart disease and bone loss in mid-life women; and the cumulative effect of low-dose exposures to environmental agents.

Faye G. Abdellah, selected in 1989-91 as the first Distinguished Research Fellow, addressed the politics of health policy formulation at the regional assemblies. Dissemination of nursing science was a major theme in the 1990s. A television program, *Nursing Approach*, featured on cable news channel CNBC, was highlighted in *Reflections*. In the spring 1991 *Reflections*, the establishment of Center Nursing Press was announced. The Sigma Theta Tau video series "Cameo: Outstanding Nurse Researchers and Their Work" was a joint venture between the society and Mosby publications. Media consultant Barbara Wallace offered members a *Media Tool Kit for Communication,* advising them that when telling a story about nursing, always conclude with the phrase "The nurse made a difference."

As part of a knowledge dissemination initiative, overviews of clinical research were published in *Reflections.* The first award for research dissemination was given at the biennial convention in 1993. Feature articles about members whose practices improved the health status of people worldwide were also published.

By the mid-1990s, each issue was oriented around a theme. As the society prepared for its 75th anniversary, scholarly articles on the values of Sigma Theta Tau International—love, courage, and honor—were published in *Reflections.* Jesus Encarnacion shared his nursing postage stamp collection, which documented a global story of heroism, knowledge, and mercy. Feature articles and research studies in the first quarter 1996 issue highlighted the heroism and courage of nurses who aided devastated communities after Hurricane Andrew hit southern Florida. Nurses who assisted victims and survivors of the Oklahoma City bombing, the 1988 Armenian earthquake, and the 1995 collapse of the Sampoong department store in Seoul, Korea, also were featured.

Barbara Wallace taught nurses the essence of being media savvy in the first quarter 1999 issue of *Reflections.*

Nurses featured on postage stamps from around the world. (Second quarter 1998).

The first quarter 1996 issue featured nurses reacting and healing in the presence of disasters. The Red Cross, the US surgeon general's office, and various nursing schools used this issue when teaching disaster preparedness and responsiveness.

Articles in *Reflections* brought the society into the information age, acquainting members with advances in the use of electronic databases, lexicons and taxonomies to categorize nursing knowledge; electronic bulletin boards; *The Online Journal of Knowledge Synthesis for Nursing;* and an online library to promote scholarship and network scholars worldwide. The Virginia Henderson International Nursing Library, conceptualized as a knowledge bank, linked taxonomies of research to the directory—later the repository—of nurse researchers, provided abstracts of research meetings and conferences, and catalogued the work of Sigma Theta Tau International's grant recipients. The beauty of it was that anyone with access to a computer and the Internet could visit the electronic library.

The Online Journal of Knowledge Synthesis for Nursing (OJKSN) became the cornerstone of the Virginia Henderson International Nursing Library. *OJKSN* was dedicated to knowledge synthesis—gathering research studies on a topic, assessing the validity of findings, and asserting implications for practice. The first editor, Jane Barnsteiner (1993), described the difficulty nurses have in staying abreast of research findings:

> Locating and gathering information on a topic of interest; organizing, summarizing, and interpreting it; and then determining the practice implications are often overwhelming and certainly time-consuming tasks. Yet they are necessary activities if our practice is to be research based and our research is to be built on a foundation of what has come before (p. 8).

The Virginia Henderson International Nursing Library was revolutionary when launched and dedicated and still is today.

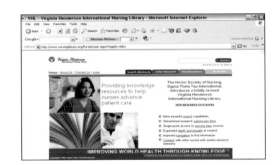

The Virginia Henderson International Nursing Library newly revamped in 2005.

Jane Barnsteiner: Pyramiding Knowledge Into Practice

By Julie Goldsmith

Photography by: Paul Crane

Parents regularly bring feverish young-sters into the emergency department at the Children's Hospital of Philadelphia. There, nurses know a parent's alarm, a child's distress. Bringing comfort and treatment to the children has not been enough for these emergency room nurses. They have expanded their base for practice with families who have a child with a fever.

"Many parents don't know how to take a temperature or know when a fever needs to be treated" says Children's Hospital's Jane Barnsteiner, RN, PhD, FAAN. They bring a child who is active and alert to the emergency department with a temperature of 100°F. Using the wealth of research that indicates most fevers are treated only if the child is symptomatic, the nursing staff have developed and are implementing a research based teaching protocol with families.

Evidence that knowledge is being communicated, transcribed and applied is a sign of changing times in health care delivery. Ten years ago, when Dr. Barnsteiner was appointed Director of Nursing Practice and Research at Children's Hospital, there was little nursing research being conducted and little translation of research findings into practice.

Dr. Barnsteiner is the pioneer editor of Sigma Theta Tau International's new *The Online Journal of Knowledge Synthesis for Nursing*, which transmits, via computer linkages, the latest research applied to nursing practice. Her work at Children's Hospital describes the adventure of today's nursing scholarship. As editor, she helps nurses at a variety of hospitals and institutions as they prepare research for publication in the journal.

She typifies nurse leaders who creatively combine several posts. In addition to her editorship of the journal and her position at Children's Hospital, Dr. Barnsteiner is associate professor and director of the pediatric critical care graduate program at the University of Pennsylvania School of Nursing.

As an example of the work she inspires at Children's Hospital, a group of 25 nurses meet monthly to review the research on topics they have selected and determine any implications for nursing practice at the institution. In addition to the review of research on fevers, synthesis topics underway this year include conscious sedation, preparation of the skin for drawing cultures, and sibling visitation. From such a review came the development of new family education materials on treatment of fevers. The synthesized knowledge along with directions for practice and research is the type of material being published in *Knowledge Synthesis for Nursing.*

"Our model of nursing practice at Children's Hospital is shaped like a pyramid. At the base of the pyramid is research, so that research and knowledge are, as much as possible, the basis

Jane Barnsteiner is featured in the summer 1994 issue of *Reflections.*

for all nursing care that is delivered. Out of research comes the directions for nursing practice," says Dr. Barnsteiner. For her work in fostering research-based practice, Dr. Barnsteiner received the Utilization of Research in Nursing Practice Regional Award from Sigma Theta Tau International in 1988.

Nursing staff, Dr. Barnsteiner believes, should participate in determining what their practice will look like. Hence she oversees a number of clinical programs that involve the participation of more than 100 staff nurses. Activities include conducting research projects, research utilization, developing, instituting and monitoring clinical programs for the establishment of standards, patient and family education materials, and quality improvement.

Dr. Barnsteiner facilitates the conduct of research by a number of clinicians in the institution. Seven research presentations and 13 poster presentations were part of "Nursing Research Day: Putting Clinical Research into Practice" held as part of 1994 Nurse Week activities at Children's Hospital.

Research done in clinical settings by clinicians is tied to the questions and problems experienced in the institution. "We are not testing major nursing concepts, but rather looking at the problems we experience in everyday nursing practice. Nurses determine if there is any current knowledge to guide their practice. If not, they will conduct studies to try and determine answers," Dr. Barnsteiner states.

By comparison, at the University of Pennsylvania School of Nursing, major programs of nursing research are carried out, generating new theories with wide scale testing and replications necessitating external funding. She cites the work of Dorothy Brooten, Jacqueline Fawcett and Barbara Lowrey as examples.

Dr. Barnsteiner's insistent curiosity is matched with disarming amounts of enthusiasm. Both of these qualities have served her well. She was the first person in her family to go to college. Growing up in Philadelphia, her mother was a bank clerk who raised seven children by herself.

Neither parent discussed the importance of education, yet Dr. Barnsteiner recalls always wanting to be a nurse from her earliest recollections. Her family life did help construct and embolden her sisterly concern for the well being of others.

With two brothers and four sisters, Dr. Barnsteiner was the fifth child. Along with the baby-sitting that was inherent in the job of being a big sister to her younger brother and sister, she worked her way through high school as a waitress, and took an extra job in a photo development factory.

"Before knowledge can be used, it must be compiled and classified in a meaningful way with the user in mind,"

In 1966, she graduated with a diploma in nursing from Misericordia Hospital School of Nursing in Philadelphia and went to work as a staff nurse in the Infant Intensive Care Unit at Children's Hospital of Philadelphia. There she took care of the first human receiving Total Parenteral Nutrition. "Being involved in the care of this infant and following the research protocol is what sparked my beginning interest in research" stated Dr. Barnsteiner.

"I was blessed with having a number of mentors," she explained. Her sister-in-law, Joan Ogden Herman, was a nurse anesthetist who encouraged her as she graduated with her diploma to enroll in a baccalaureate program. During her diploma schooling, Regina Wielga, the assistant director of the program, encouraged her to ask questions, not be afraid to do things differently, and to pursue graduate study.

Dr. Barnsteiner obtained her bachelor's degree in nursing in 1970 and her master's degree in maternal and child health in 1973, both from the University of Pennsylvania. She then returned to Children's Hospital where she was by her own assessment a "young whipper snapper". Her mentor, then Nursing Director Erna Goulding, allowed her to ask questions and challenge the old ways of doing things — despite the sometimes nervous reactions it caused throughout the institution.

As Assistant Director for Clinical Nursing, Dr. Barnsteiner identified questions in the delivery of care that had never been studied: positioning, suctioning, effects of family participation in care. "We were doing care based on tradition and not based on knowledge," she says.

Her desire to know more about how to study children's responses motivated her to seek a doctoral degree. Dr. Barnsteiner earned her PhD in clinical nursing research from the University of Michigan and then accepted the partnership position as a Clinician Educator at the Children's Hospital and the University of Pennsylvania School of Nursing.

The relationship of practice to research has been more than her own individual pathway to knowledge. It is nursing's real present and future.

At Sigma Theta Tau International's 31st Biennial Convention, Dr. Barnsteiner delivered the keynote address on Research Day, eliciting rounds of applause for her sentiments on the subject.

"Before knowledge can be used, it must be compiled and classified in a meaningful way with the user in mind," she said. She believes every person should graduate from a nursing program with an understanding of how to translate research findings into practice protocols and diffuse them through the system. Encouraging nurse researchers to assist clinicians, Dr. Barnsteiner said practitioners need support in assessing if care is based on current knowledge.

"The measure of leadership in nursing research is not the quality of the head but the tone of the body," she said expanding on a quote by Max DePree. "Therefore, signs of research leadership will appear among the work of practitioners. The evidence of nursing leadership will be the existence of research-based practices, which indicate that practitioners are getting access to knowledge and using it." ∎

In the fall of 1994, it was reported in *Reflections* that 13 scholars working in clinical decision making and nursing judgments had gathered for the First Scholars Colloquia at the International Center for Nursing Scholarship.

As the society developed, chapter members became more interested in preserving chapter heritage. Kathryn Schweer, International Heritage Committee member, discussed the resources available to chapters, especially the "Guidelines for Chapter Historical Materials." To support this effort, a column on the preservation of a scholarly legacy was published in *Reflections*.

International nurse researchers.

In 1993, the honor society partnered with other organizations to double the amount of research awards. By 1995, there were three corporate sponsors and five collaborative sponsors.

Growing Into an International Organization

In the spring 1990 issue of *Reflections*, international schools and members were included in the list of new nursing doctorates. The fall 1995 issue reported preliminary findings from Connie Baker's global comparison of nursing doctoral programs from 27 countries. In June 1995, there were 62 nursing doctoral programs around the world.

A collaborative International Nursing Research Conference with the theme Voyage Into the Future Through Nursing Research, sponsored by 10 Ohio schools of nursing and nine Sigma Theta Tau International chapters, welcomed researchers from 22 countries to Columbus, OH, in May 1992.

In 1993, Sigma Theta Tau International joined with three universities in the Netherlands to sponsor an international research meeting. Research conferences were also held that year during the 20th Quadrennial Congress of the International Council of Nurses (ICN) in Spain and in Egypt following the ICN meeting. The theme of the Egyptian conference was Ethical Issues and Health Care. In 1994, Sydney, Australia, became the site of the Seventh International Nursing Research Congress, with the theme The Adventures of Nursing Practice Through Research. The Royal College of Nursing, Australia, and Sigma Theta Tau International co-sponsored the conference. A study tour of Australia, New Zealand, and the Great Barrier Reef was arranged for after the meeting.

The Ninth International Research Conference was held in 1997 in concert with the 21st Quadrennial Congress of the ICN in Vancouver, Canada. The University of Utrecht's Department

At the 1998 Research Congress in the Netherlands.

of Nursing Science, The University of Ghent's Department of Public Health, Pace University's Lienhard School of Nursing, and Sigma Theta Tau International hosted the 10th International Nursing Research Congress in July 1998. The theme for the meeting was Nursing Research for a Changing World.

Lucie Kelly's "International Nursing News" column reported on international research and provided a forum for the growing worldwide membership. *Reflections* also featured reports from correspondents in the US, Australia, Asia, Middle East, Europe, Eastern Europe, Central America, and Jamaica.

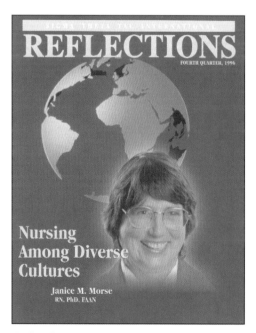

In the third quarter 1998 issue of *Reflections*, Susie Kim talks about advocating for the mentally ill in South Korea.

Nurse Syringa Marshall-Burnett, Jamaica's senate president, was featured as a "Change Maker" in the fourth quarter 1998 issue of *Reflections*.

Reflections begins a series of features related to global nursing. In the fourth quarter 1996 issue, Janice Morse brings a new awareness to cultural sensitivity.

In 1996 and 1997, clinical and research studies from international and cross-cultural perspectives were featured in *Reflections*. These articles presented a study of beliefs about family planning among Khmer emigres to Canada, the medication usage of elderly people in two northern Taiwan communities, comparisons of birth experiences of Australian and Vietnamese mothers in Australia, and the effects of war on health care in Rwanda in the 1990s. Members and schools of nursing used *Reflections* to discuss their academic and scholarly exchange programs; many authors described nursing educational systems outside the US.

Reflections covers the changing needs of Cambodian emigres to Canada.

Reflections tackles the difficult topic of Taiwanese elderly and their adherence—or not—to prescription recommendations.

For example, Marla Salmon quoted articles one and two of the United Nations' 1948 Universal Declaration of Human Rights as a framework for the development of civilization and good societies around the world. She highlighted the efforts of nurses around the world who work for justice.

Mi Ja Kim, a wisdom figure among Korean nurses, wrote a column for the 75th anniversary issue, stating that the bellwether standard for research should be its effect on policies, actions, and the treatment of patients. She urged interdisciplinary research because of the complexity of problems and encouraged international nurses to join in policy development.

In 1998, President Eleanor Sullivan wrote a message on commitment to global health, emphasizing that Sigma Theta Tau International was a global organization, even though only 3,000 of 124,000 members lived outside the US. Increasingly since 1988, the society has emphasized strengthening its global diversity through engagement of members from across the globe on committees and councils. Beginning in 1996, issues of *Reflections* have been identified by quarters as opposed to seasons, because of the difference in seasons around the world.

As the society approached the millennium, it partnered with the World Health Organization (WHO) and the ICN to share knowledge, organizational initiatives, print materials, and access to Web sites.

Melanie Dreher called global sharing another example of the futuristic and magnanimous approach to healthcare that has become Sigma Theta Tau International's signature.

Philanthropy

Lucie Kelly reported that the Knowledge Building Campaign had achieved $4 million in gifts and pledges and was close to achieving its $4.6 million goal. By the winter 1991 issue, it was announced that $5 million had been raised to support the International Center for Nursing Scholarship and the International Library.

"The spirit of philanthropy was imbedded in the society's structure."

Sigma Theta Tau International announced its second capital campaign in 1991 at the biennial convention in Tampa, FL. This $7.5 million campaign would support the Library Endowment, Leadership Fund, Sustaining Annual Fund, Friends of the Library Fund, Presidential Chain Fund, and the celebration itself. In the fall 1995 issue of *Reflections*, it was reported that the 75th anniversary campaign had exceeded $3.6 million. Honorary member Rosemary Crisp was named chair, and Glenn Irwin was appointed to lead the campaign. Beverly Booker and Adele Hall, community leaders from Kansas City, and James Delusion from Texas were also on the committee.

Nancy Dickenson-Hazard and Melanie Dreher cut the cake to celebrate hitting the halfway mark on the 75th anniversary fund-raising drive.

In 1996, Dreher cut the celebration cake as the 75th anniversary campaign passed the halfway mark. By the end of the year, the campaign had reached $5.4 million, 72% of its goal. At the biennial birthday celebration, it was announced that the campaign had received $8.5 million in gifts and pledges.

Two new development ventures were initiated early in the 1990s: The Friends of the Library, chaired by former President Vernice Ferguson, and the Annual Fund. A $1 million goal to support the library was announced during the presidency of Beth Vaughan-Wrobel.

Audrey Hepburn Lauded for Caring

PHOTOS BY HAROLD MILLER

Audrey Hepburn, a long-time UNICEF champion, was presented with the first Sigma Theta Tau International Lifetime Achievement Award in 1992.

In the spring of 1991, Luther Christman and his colleague, Sheldon Garber, from Rush University, recommended that resource development be added to goals of knowledge development, dissemination, and utilization. The spirit of philanthropy was imbedded in the society's structure.

Audrey Hepburn received the first Sigma Theta Tau International Lifetime Achievement Award in 1992 for her work with UNICEF on behalf of the children of the world.

In the 1990s, members who committed $25,000 or more to the society as a gift, pledge, or planned gift became Virginia Henderson Fellows (the contribution amount has changed since that time). Issues of *Reflections* included portraits and profiles of the philanthropists. By 1999, there were 200 Virginia Henderson Fellows.

In the mid-1990s, the society promoted a Scholars' Travel Club. The first meeting was a Caribbean Christmas cruise; the second was a trip to New York City. Promoted as a reasonably priced travel and educational adventure, the club was an effort to increase member engagement in the spirit of philanthropy. These new events were reported in *Reflections*, as were follow-up stories of their success.

Virginia Henderson Fellows

The Scholars' Travel Club

The Helene Fuld Trust Fund awarded Sigma Theta Tau International $176,000 to test a new learning model—the value and application of concept maps to particular domains of nursing. The maps were generated by the honor society's knowledge indexes.

In 1996, the Hugoton Foundation invested $75,000 in the Leadership Institute to commemorate the 75th anniversary of Sigma Theta Tau International.

The Billye Brown Society was established in 1999 to recognize members who make planned gifts to benefit the international society or chapters. Brown so clearly exemplified the nurse philanthropist that Eleanor Sullivan characterized her as the mother of Sigma Theta Tau International fund raising.

The Center for Nursing Scholarship

The mission of the society was enlivened on Jan. 2, 1990, with the opening of the International Center for Nursing Scholarship and the International Nursing Library. Carole Hudgings was named library director, and June Abbey chaired the first International Nursing Library scientific committee.

Articles in *Reflections* allowed members who could not visit Indianapolis to take a virtual tour of the center and the state-of-the-art library. The library was envisioned as an electronic gateway designed to distribute information to nurses worldwide.

Susan Sparks of the National Library of Medicine created a book of 100 historical nursing photographs from 1850-1960. This book was presented at the center's

Focusing on information technology in 1990.

dedication by David Lindberg, director of the National Library of Medicine.

The spring 1992 issue of *Reflections,* dedicated to the Virginia Henderson International Nursing Library, presented the plan for the library and *The Online Journal of Knowledge Synthesis for Nursing.* Judith Graves, who had provided leadership and inspiration for the Virginia Henderson International Nursing Library, was featured on the cover of the spring 1993 issue.

In the second quarter of 1996, the technology revolution and its impact on clinical innovation and care outcomes were examined in *Reflections.* Reports of clinical research profiled the work of members as they created computerized emergency drug cards, documented critical-care nursing practice, and developed an online program to identify patients susceptible to falls. Researchers at Ann Arbor, MI, used video conferencing software called CU-See Me to study whether keeping in touch with friends and families had an effect on patient recovery. Telemedicine helped nurses in rural communities monitor their patients and retool their assessment skills. Educators described how online technologies brought programs of nursing education to rural communities. Korean members explained how the enactment of national health insurance in Korea increased patient demand and the

Judith Graves helped make the Virginia Henderson International Nursing Library the pre-eminent nursing library.

Nurses at the forefront of the technology explosion of the 1990s.

Nurses proving the healing power of keeping connected.

development of better clinical and nursing information management systems. The Virginia Henderson International Nursing Library, perched on the edge of the technology explosion, was showcased as a service to the nursing profession.

Kathleen Stevens, chair of the International Library Committee, said the library and the online journal put science at your fingertips.

When Graves announced her retirement in the second quarter of 1996, she described the beginnings of the Virginia Henderson International Nursing Library, noting that the initial work was to move databases, as the *Registry of Nursing Research*, from paper to electronic format to the Internet. The library began to collect and scan abstracts from selected regional, national, and international meetings, and doctoral graduates were asked to submit surveys and dissertation abstracts, which became the dissertation database. The society digitized data from grant recipients, as well, and the table of contents of each *Image* (now *Journal of Nursing Scholarship*) and Sigma Theta Tau International monographs were also added.

The Virginia Henderson International Nursing Library added two significant elements to its research classification system in 1998: a list of research-oriented and specialty practice associations—including the US military, the US Department of Health and Human Services, and the Veterans Administration—and the addition of study descriptors to programs of research.

No one can be too poor, old, or sick for a nurse's healing gift and power of hope.

Julie Goldsmith Reflects Back

Some 300 e-mails from nurses flash across my computer screen daily, while ambulance sirens cry beneath my window overlooking the avenue to nearby emergency departments. Nurses, at the forefront of unending tragedies and limitless solutions, are always on my mind.

In 1991, Nell Watts, executive director of Sigma Theta Tau International, invited me to turn the organizational newsletter into a newsmagazine with the support of nurses throughout the world. *Reflections* reached out to all areas of nursing—to scholars in Africa, Australia, Europe, the Americas, and even the Arctic—to report on best practices in 70 nations.

Virginia Henderson, herself, guided me in my second month on the job, impressing upon me the essential ties between research and practice, when we met in Tampa, FL. Sr. Rosemary Donley, Luther Christman, Angela Barron McBride, Imogene King, and Vernice Ferguson were some of the nursing visionaries whose scopes of knowledge helped us reflect innovations of nurses. The elected international presidents fine-tuned the magazine to meet global nursing needs at the time by spurring stories on leadership, evidence-based practices, or cultural competencies, for example.

While not formally peer-reviewed, *Reflections* benefited from the intellectual capital and advice of 50 to 75 nursing scholars per issue, all of whom informally directed us. As a result, *Reflections* was accepted into the scientific indexing resources of MEDLINE and CINAHL, with the help of informaticist Judith Graves.

In the mid-1990s, executive officer Nancy Dickenson-Hazard raised the magazine's publication and printing values, giving *Reflections* a glossier, more professional finish. Until then, nurses donated most photographs. These changes allowed us to give visual heart to nurses' stories. Never before had any magazine published so many diverse photos of nurses. Dickenson-Hazard also initiated a regular section with poems written by nurses about nursing.

The impact of the magazine grew. A *Reflections* feature about nursing in disasters told the stories of how nurses managed wide-scale tragedies and chaos. The American Red Cross and the office of the U.S. surgeon general began using this issue of *Reflections* in their emergency training sessions. Schools of nursing and hospitals plied us with requests to reprint *Reflections* for educational purposes. Another feature, about nursing across the life span, was sent to all members of the U.S. Congress by the National Institute of Nursing Research. Hospitals throughout the world asked us to reprint Neville Strumpf's and Lois Evans' research on restraint-free care of the elderly. Institutions and governing bodies changed their regulations as a result of this article. We received accolades from journalism groups and from nursing's own—the media award from the American Academy of Nursing. With Betty Ferrell's help, we examined best practices for end-of-life care, and physicians and other professionals couldn't get enough extra copies. We ran to the photocopier and wrote blanket permissions to reprint.

continued

Nurses leading the way underpinned the stories. Syringa Marshall Burnett, featured on one cover, rose to high elected office in Jamaica, partly as a result of solving the housing problems in her nation after hurricanes. Susie Kim, whose research on schizophrenia was funded by the United Nations, was on a cover after her wide-scale study in South Korea benefited people who had been without hope.

Some stories told of nurses who founded solar-powered health clinics in mountains of Nicaragua, AIDS clinics in Denver, urban clinics in Milwaukee, and birthing centers in Malawi. Nurses designed culturally competent practices for Inuit residents in Canada and Afghanis in San Francisco.

We also looked at the past and told the story of the rise of nursing science, journeying through wars, epidemics, hospitals and higher education with the counsel of Joan Lynaugh and other eminent historians.

Hundreds of nurses reflected the many-sided pursuit for social equity in health care. No one can be too poor, old, or sick for a nurse's healing gift and power of hope. *Reflections* has always celebrated this legacy.

Julie Goldsmith, MSJ, an independent journalist, was editor of Reflections *from 1991 to 2000. She is in doctoral school at Michigan State University, College of Communication Arts and Sciences.*

Entering the New Millennium: 2000-2005

AS PRESIDENT DURING the 1999-2001 biennium, Patricia E. Thompson led the Honor Society of Nursing, Sigma Theta Tau International into the 21st century with the call to action Learning & Leading Globally. At this time, the honor society had 406 chapters in 75 countries on six continents. It was time to solidify and build upon the gains the honor society had made in the 1990s toward becoming a truly global organization.

During this biennium, Strategic Plan 2005 was implemented, based on a vision to "create a global community of nurses …" and a mission to "support the learning and professional development of our members, who strive to improve nursing

Pat Thompson featured in the first quarter 2001 issue.

Strategic planning for the new millennium.

Chiron participants gather during the first Chiron program retreat.

care worldwide" (Strategic Plan 2005, p. 55). The plan identified seven goals for the first five years of the new millennium, with an emphasis in 1999-2001 on the first two goals: developing members across their lifespans and building strong chapters and fostering collaborative leadership.

In 2000, six mentors and fellows launched a new program called Chiron: The Mentor-Fellow Forum. Named for Chiron, the centaur in Western mythology that mentored Aesculapius, Achilles, and Hercules, this new International Leadership Institute program offered members the opportunity to develop leadership skills as a fellow, mentor, or senior fellow.

The Arista series of think-tank meetings was another initiative of the International Leadership Institute. Arista brought together an interdisciplinary expert panel, and reactors were invited to converse, debate, explain, and develop strategies for the future of nursing. Arista3 meetings, held from 2001-2003, focused on specific regions of the world—Americas, Pacific region, Europe, Africa and Near East, and Italy.

In addition to Arista3, Patricia Thompson encouraged other global initiatives: (a) development of the International Academic Nursing Alliance (IANA); (b) establishment of a partnership with the American International Health Alliance (AIHA) to promote leadership development of nurses in Central and Eastern Europe and the former Soviet Union; and (c) international chapter development, especially in Asia and the Pacific Rim.

Special initiatives to promote the growth and development of members and chapter leaders also were launched during the 1999-2001 biennium. Redesigned regional conferences, now called Professional Development Conferences and Chapter Leader Academies, offered members and chapter leaders educational tracks on important topics, such as achieving career goals, volunteering, becoming funded researchers, and living life as a chapter leader.

Reflecting Back

The magazine itself changed in significant ways during this biennium. Beginning with the first quarter of 2000, the name was changed to *Reflections on Nursing Leadership* to more accurately reflect the magazine's content and purpose.

In the third quarter 2001 issue, Editor James E. Mattson introduced a new feature, "Reflecting Back," a retrospective piece on a selected aspect of the honor society or nursing, located inside the magazine's back cover. The first "Reflecting Back" focused on the evolution of the member newsmagazine from a four-page,

Participants of the Arista3 Pacific-Rim think tank.

Participants of the Africa and Near East Arista3 Group.

The first "Reflecting Back" column was published in the third quarter 2001 issue.

Reflecting Back ...

become a NURSE
YOUR COUNTRY NEEDS YOU
Write Nursing Information Bureau, 1790 Broadway, New York City

"Reflecting Back" looks back on a nurse recruiting poster from 1942.

reading

Reflections on Nursing Leadership begins publishing book reviews in the first quarter 2001 issue.

one-color newsletter to a glossy, full-color format. The fourth quarter 2001 issue featured a cadet nurse recruitment poster from 1942, reminding us that the current nursing shortage is not the first.

Another First: Book Reviews

Another new feature in *Reflections on Nursing Leadership* began in first quarter 2001 with the review of a Sigma Theta Tau International book, *Cadet Nurse Stories*. The reviews of recently published or forthcoming books raised members' awareness of the latest books from the publications area, then known as Center Nursing Press. Beginning with the publication of *Making a Difference: Stories From the Point of Care* in May 2000, the honor society began to dramatically increase the number and type of books published.

36th Biennial Convention

Among highlights of the honor society's 36th Biennial Convention in Indianapolis, IN, in 2001 was Rosalynn Carter's acceptance of the Sigma Theta Tau International Lifetime Achievement Award. Carter, a former first lady of the US, received the honor for her efforts over more than 30 years to improve the quality of life for people around the world. An advocate for mental health at The Carter Center in

Atlanta, GA, she also supported early childhood immunization, human rights, conflict resolution, and empowerment of urban communities. During the Carter administration, the first lady served as honorary chair of the President's Commission on Mental Health, which resulted in passage of the Mental Health Systems Act of 1980.

Building Diverse Relationships

President May L. Wykle's call to action for the 2001-2003 biennium was Building Diverse Relationships. Wykle (2002) encouraged members to think about diversity in the broadest sense, taking advantage of the multifaceted nature of the honor society's global membership: "The richness these diverse individuals bring to the work of the organization will strengthen our outcomes in achieving the strategies of the biennial call to action" (p. 51).

Evidence-Based Practice

Evidence-based practice (EBP) became a growing area of emphasis beginning with the 1998-1999 strategic planning process, which led to the establishment of an Evidence-Based Nursing Task Force in 2000. The task force developed a plan and an impressive series of outcomes that were highlighted in the second quarter 2002 issue of *Reflections on Nursing Leadership*.

Rosalynn Carter is honored with the Lifetime Achievement Award at the 2001 biennial convention.

May Wykle featured in the first quarter 2002 issue of *Reflections on Nursing Leadership*.

Updating members on EBN efforts.

***Worldviews on Evidence-Based Nursing*
was launched in March 2004.**

Issues in the second and fourth quarters of 2002 included several articles defining evidence-based nursing and focusing on the use of evidence in improving health status and care delivery around the world.

In December 2002, the honor society issued a position statement on evidence-based nursing (EBN). In the same month, the board of directors decided the honor society should develop a cutting-edge journal on EBN. After intense planning in 2003, a new peer-reviewed, quarterly journal, *Worldviews on Evidence-Based Nursing*, was launched in March 2004. Published by Blackwell Publishing on behalf of the honor society. *Worldviews* is led by an international editorial team of EBN experts, with Jo Rycroft-Malone (UK) as editor and Tracey Bucknall (Australia) and Bernadette Mazurek Melnyk (US) as associate editors. The international editorial advisory board is comprised of EBN experts from every region of the world. Integrative reviews that previously had been published in the honor society's *Online Journal of Knowledge Synthesis for Nursing (OJKSN)* became an archive of *Worldviews on Evidence-Based Nursing* in June 2004.

Creating the Future Through Renewal

President Daniel J. Pesut began his 2003-2005 term with the call to action Create the
Future Through Renewal. Pesut (2004), the honor society's first male president,
encouraged all honor society members to:

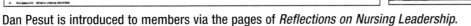

Dan Pesut is introduced to members via the pages of *Reflections on Nursing Leadership.*

Ready to create the future through renewal? Here are some ideas ...

■ Complete a VIP Profile. ■ Complete a CareeRxel™ program. ■ Offer expertise to the global community. ■ Submit an abstract to present at research programs. ■ Volunteer translation services for honor society documents. ■ Start a book club using honor society publications. ■ Learn about the scholarly work of experts on reflective practice. ■ Nominate chapter members for international award recognition. ... **These are just eight of the more than 150 ways** you or your chapter can respond to President Daniel Pesut's 2003-2005 call to action. Find more idea stimulators by visiting **www.nursingsociety.org**.

Dan Pesut utilized many avenues within *Reflections on Nursing Leadership* **to communicate the 2003-2005 "Create the Future Through Renewal," including completing your VIProfile (right).**

Spend some time in this biennium focusing attention on what you believe and value in regard to renewal of self, service, the scholarship of reflective practice, science, society and spirit in your sphere of influence. Act on what is meaningful and doable for yourself and your chapter (p. 57).

He provided members with several ideas on how to create the future through renewal, including completing the new Web-based Volunteer Interest Profile, or VIProfile, and exploring CareeRxel™, the honor society's online career development program.

Mentoring was another millennium theme. In fact, it became a mantra in *Reflections on Nursing Leadership*. The magazine depicted how the concept developed into a research and practice agenda and provided a forum for members to discuss the mentor-protégé relationship, explore its underlying values of mutual trust and respect, and plot its impact on leadership succession, success and satisfaction. Connie Vance, who in the 1980s introduced mentoring into the nursing literature, reflected on the characteristics of the mentor: generosity, competence, self-confidence, and openness to mutuality; and the characteristics of the protégé: initiative, career commitment, self-identity, and openness to mutuality.

Reflections on Nursing Leadership also honored nurses who made a difference in global health. The third quarter 2000 issue featured two recipients of the International Florence Nightingale medal: Marie Lysnes of Norway and Maria Petursdottir of Iceland.

The magazine highlighted global themes of the millennium: the technology explosion and its implications for nursing practice, education and research; terrorism; societal aging and its clinical and ethical implications; the nursing shortage and the quality of the international workforce and workplace; global and universal access to health care; and delivery of care to underserved populations of the world.

Other themes were multidisciplinary and international collaboration, nurse management of HIV/AIDS, evidence-based practice around the world, nontraditional and multifaceted roles of nurses in contemporary health delivery systems, social and health policy, and the Magnet hospital movement. Cross-cultural comparisons presented the regulation of registered nursing in the US, Canada, Southeast Asia, and Western Pacific.

The Magnet Recognition Program is an example of what the nursing profession can create and accomplish in the midst of crisis.
— *Kammie Monarch*

Kammie Monarch, chief operating officer for Sigma Theta Tau International, traces the Magnet movement in the fourth quarter 2003 issue of *Reflections on Nursing Leadership.*

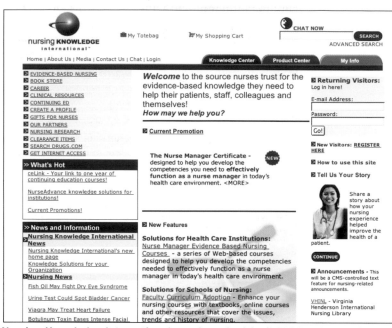

Nursing Knowledge International was launched April 2004 and recently updated based upon member and user feedback.

Luther Christman and Imogene King, both longtime honor society members, celebrating their inductions into the American Nurses Association Hall of Fame in 2004.

Important Milestones and Achievements in 2004 and 2005

Nursing Knowledge International (NKI), a subsidiary of Sigma Theta Tau International, was launched in April 2004 as a Web-based nursing portal, www.nursingknowledge.org, to provide nurse-centric professional development and knowledge solutions from the honor society. Associations and for-profit companies formed partnerships to serve the informational needs of honor society members and the global nursing community.

Reflections on Nursing Leadership received five awards for graphic design and editorial excellence in 2005 and two in 2004 from APEX and Magnum Opus. These awards can be directly attributed to the magazine's editor, James Mattson, who has a unique combination of skills that allow him to handle both the design and layout and editorial content of the magazine. The cover-story profile of US Surgeon General Richard H. Carmona in the first quarter 2005 issue, titled "Been There, Done That," received the 2005 APEX Award for Excellence: Personality Profile and the 2005 Magnum Opus Honorable Mention: Best Interview or Profile, as well as an Honorable Mention from the Media Awards Committee of the American Academy of Nursing in 2005.

Sigma Theta Tau International members Luther Christman and Imogene King were inducted into the American Nurses Association (ANA) Hall of Fame at the ANA biennial convention in June 2004.

Nancy Dickenson-Hazard celebrated her 10th anniversary as chief executive officer of Sigma Theta Tau International with a scrapbook of memories presented to her at the annual holiday party held at headquarters in December 2004.

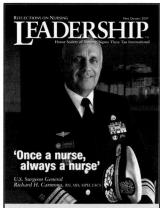

CEO marks 10 years

Dan Pesut and Nancy Dickenson-Hazard, the honor society's president and chief executive officer, respectively, look through a scrapbook that staff members presented to Dickenson-Hazard to celebrate her 10th anniversary at the helm of Sigma Theta Tau International. During that decade, the number of chapters burgeoned from 324 to 423, and the number of inducted members grew from 190,000 to more than 345,000. The scrapbook was presented to Dickenson-Hazard during the annual holiday party held at headquarters.

Nancy Dickenson-Hazard and Dan Pesut look over the scrapbook Nancy received from Sigma Theta Tau International staff members to honor her 10th anniversary as chief executive officer of the honor society.

RNL *receives five awards for writing and design excellence*

Reflections on Nursing Leadership (*RNL*) was recently awarded five awards for excellence in writing and design.

In June, the magazine received two APEX Awards for Publication Excellence in a competition sponsored by Communications Concepts, Inc., one for design and layout, the other for the cover story "Been there, done that," a profile of U.S. Surgeon General Richard H. Carmona authored by James Mattson, editor of the magazine. The article appeared in the First Quarter 2005 issue of *RNL*. A total of 757 entries were submitted in the competition.

In July, *RNL* received three Magnum Opus awards for outstanding achievement: 1) Silver Award for Best Overall Editorial, recognition of the magazine's excellent content; 2) Honorable Mention for Best Overall Design; and 3) Honorable Mention for Best Interview or Profile, also for the cover story about U.S. Surgeon General Carmona.

The Magnum Opus award competition, sponsored by Publications Management, attracted more than 500 entries. Professors from the Missouri School of Journalism and leading custom-publishing professionals issued the awards based on specific criteria. Using a 0-50 scale for each criterion, they considered such elements as information value, quality of writing and display, use of imagery and typography, and consistency of color palette and style. In addition to selecting Gold, Silver and Bronze winners and a Grand Magnum Opus Award in each of nine categories, up to three honorable mentions were selected in each category.

In 2004, *Reflections on Nursing Leadership* received two APEX Awards of Excellence, one for design and layout, the other for writing.

"Award-winning" isn't just a catch-phrase. In 2005, *Reflections on Nursing Leadership* received two APEX awards, one for design and layout and the other for the cover story "Been There, Done That," a profile of Surgeon General Richard H. Carmona. A month later, the magazine was awarded three Magnum Opus awards for outstanding achievement: (1) Silver Award for Best Overall Editorial, recognition of the magazine's excellent content; (2) Honorable Mention for Best Overall Design; and (3) Honorable Mention for Best Interview or Profile, also for the cover story about US Surgeon General Carmona.

Nell J. Watts, legendary nursing leader and honor society executive officer from 1974-1993, was remembered in *Reflections on Nursing Leadership* after her passing in 2005.

Elizabeth Dole and Luci Baines Johnson co-chaired Nursing Image Coalition, a collaborative effort of 18 organizations, to promote "Nurses for a Healthier Tomorrow," a comprehensive public relations program to address the nursing shortage.

Nell J. Watts, the honor society's visionary executive officer from 1974 to 1993, passed away on Feb. 28, 2005.

The redesigned and enhanced electronic Virginia Henderson International Nursing Library was launched in July 2005. The ultimate goal of the library, accessed at www.nursinglibrary.org, is to be one of the most comprehensive and current resources of nursing information. The library and its complementary database, the *Registry of Nursing Research,* provide free access to up-to-date nursing research data in studies submitted by researchers and in conference abstracts collected from organizations sponsoring nursing research meetings.

The Future of *Reflections on Nursing Leadership* is Now

Over the past 30 years, the honor society's magazine has evolved from a four-page, one-color newsletter, the initial purpose of which was to promote better communication between Sigma Theta Tau International and its members and chapters, to a full-color, award-winning newsmagazine that features stories documenting the extraordinary contributions that honor society members and other nurses are making on the front lines of healthcare around the world.

Going forward, the publication continues to evolve. With the third quarter 2005 issue, an online site was launched for *Reflections on Nursing Leadership* at **www. nursingsociety/RNL.** The online version has the content and graphic appeal that honor society members have come to expect from the print magazine, but also allows instant delivery via the Internet, links to related sites and resources on the World Wide Web, and immediate dissemination to every corner of the globe. The newsmagazine continues to change to better meet members' information and knowledge needs by taking advantage of the latest advances in information technology and delivery.

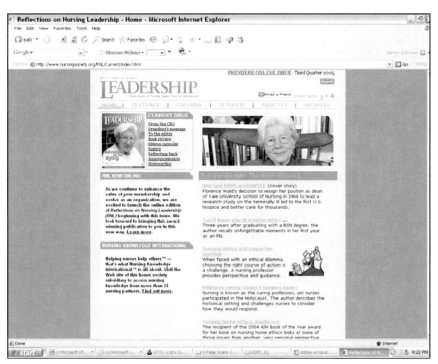

The newest evolution of *Reflections on Nursing Leadership* was launched August 2005.

Getting Better All the Time ...

As *RNL* moves to an online format, I suspect some people will miss sitting down and fingering their way through the stories. However, I am excited about the possibilities and potentials associated with stories and features that enable people to visit supplemental Web links and additional resources. With a click of the mouse, members can explore, connect, and learn more through the nursing leadership stories that are shared and circulated. The online version of *RNL* is another portal for accessing the international nursing knowledge network and building a global community of nurse leaders.

—Daniel J. Pesut, PhD, APRN, BC, FAAN

Founders

MARY TOLLE WRIGHT was born in Brownsburg, Indiana, on 14 July 1900. She graduated form Lebanon High School in Lebanon, Indiana and attended Indiana University in 1919. Mary graduated from Indiana University Training School in 1923. In 1925, she married. She had two sons, John and William. During her career, she lived in Houston, Texas, where she did private duty, general duty, and night duty. Mary lived in Little Rock, AR, for approximately 30 years. Here, she did volunteer teaching for the Red Cross and served as executive secretary for the State Nursing Association and the State Board of Nursing. She was active with the League of Nursing (now National League for Nursing [NLN]), was the director of nursing at Arkansas Baptist Hospital, and was chief nurse of the mobile blood bank. While living abroad, she was a U.S.O.M. clinic nurse in Nepal, India. Mrs. Wright's overseas travels also included living in Liberia, Nepal, and Afghanistan. She died 20 February 1999 in Weslaco, Texas.

EDITH MOORE COPELAND was born on 10 June 1901, in Brazil, Indiana. She attended Indiana University School of Nursing in 1919. On 29 June 1924 Edith married Fred Copeland; she had two sons, Fred Jr. and John Robert. As an industrial nurse, she later worked at McDonnell Aircraft in St. Louis, Missouri. After moving to California, Mrs. Copeland worked at Merritt Hospital and for three internists practicing in Oakland, California. After she retired in May 1969, she worked with the Peace Corps. She resided in San Mateo, California until her death on 5 October 1992.

MARIE HIPPENSTEEL LINGEMAN was born on 17 August 1900, in Rochester, Indiana, and graduated from high school in North Manchester, Indiana. She graduated from Indiana University School of Nursing in 1923 and married Dr. Ralph Lingeman that same year. They relocated to Ft. Lauderdale, Florida, and their family included four children. Marie's nursing career included work in general duty, as an OB supervisor, and as an office nurse for two physicians. While suffering from chronic obstructive pulmonary disease, she requested to be buried in North Manchester, Indiana. Her family became her main interest until her death on 7 September 1984.

DOROTHY GARRIGUS ADAMS was born on 23 September 1902, in Brazil, Indiana. She attended the local Brazil High School and graduated from Indiana University School of Nursing in 1924. After graduation, she was a staff nurse at: James Whitcomb Riley Hospital in Indianapolis, Indiana; at St. Louis Children's Hospital in St. Louis, Missouri; and at Edwards Hospital in Ft. Lauderdale, Florida. Dorothy served as the pediatric supervisor at City Hospital in Indianapolis, Indiana; and as administrator and director of nursing at Methodist Hospital in Princeton, Indiana. While living in Florida, she was the administrator and director of nursing at Broward General Hospital, Ft. Lauderdale, Florida; and worked for many years at Gibson General Hospital. After retiring, she moved to Boynton Beach, Florida. She died on 2 March 1969. She was married to Kenneth Adams, formerly of New York.

ELIZABETH RUSSELL BELFORD was born on 23 December 1902, in Jeffersonville, Indiana, where she graduated from public school. She attended Indiana University School of Nursing, 1920-23 and 1923-25. She married Dr. William W. Belford, pediatrician, on 8 October 1925. Her family included two daughters, Mary and Martha. She served as head nurse of the medical ward and night supervisor at St. Louis Children's Hospital, St. Louis, Missouri. After moving to California, Mrs. Belford was a director on the boards of the San Diego's Neighborhood House, the Francis W. Parker School, Children's Home, and Dodson Home for the Aged. She was also involved with San Diego's St. Paul's Episcopal Church, the University of California Hospitals Auxiliary, the Society for Crippled Children, and Mercy Hospital Auxiliary. She died from a massive heart attack on 13 October 1980.

Elizabeth McWilliams Miller was born on 29 July 1901, in Olney, Illinois. She graduated from Indiana University School of Nursing in 1922. Her family included one daughter and three sons. She was widowed in 1962, after 32 years of marriage. Mrs. Miller worked as a public health nurse in Rushville, Indiana; in Washington, D.C., and in Miami, Florida. She also conducted field research in the southeastern states area for the National Committee on the Costs of Medical Care study. Mrs. Miller also worked in the PHN program for the WPA in Dade County, Miami, Florida, and assisted in the formation of the nursing section of the Dade County Health Department. She occasionally was a relief nurse at the University of Miami Infirmary. In 1988, Sigma Theta Tau instituted a Distinguished Lecturer Award in her honor. Mrs. Miller lived in Miami, Florida, until her death on 25 November 1993.

Ethel Palmer Clarke was born in 1875 in Devon County, England. At the age of 16, she came to the United States with her family and settled in Virginia. After graduating from the University of Maryland School of Nursing in Baltimore in 1906, she served as the superintendent of the De Soto Sanitarium in Jacksonville, Florida from 1907-1911. From 1911-1914, she was superintendent of the University of Maryland Hospital in Baltimore. After attending Teachers College at Columbia University from 1914-15, she served as director of the Indiana University Training School for Nursing from 1915-1932. While director, she was instrumental to the founders while they were nursing students in 1922. Prior to her death in 1968, she lived in Clinton, Colorado. She lived to be 93 years of age.

Fact Sheet

The Honor Society of Nursing, Sigma Theta Tau International – In 1922 six nurses founded Sigma Theta Tau at the Indiana University Training School for Nurses, now the Indiana University School of Nursing, in Indianapolis, Ind. The founders chose the name from the Greek words Storgé, Tharsos and Timé meaning "love," "courage," and "honor." The honor society became incorporated in 1985 as Sigma Theta Tau International, Inc., a not-for-profit organization with a 501(c)(3) tax status in the United States.

Nursing Knowledge International - Nursing Knowledge International was established in 2002 as a nonprofit, 501(c)(3) subsidiary of the honor society to serve the knowledge needs of the global nursing community. Through its Web site, www.nursingknowledge.org, the organization delivers nursing knowledge designed to improve patient outcomes by enhancing the knowledge base of its nurse customers.

The International Honor Society of Nursing Building Corporation – The Building Corporation, incorporated in 1993 as a corporation with 501(c)(2) status, holds title to real and personal property for the benefit of Sigma Theta Tau International. The Building Corporation also manages and maintains the honor society's 39,350 square foot building and grounds.

Sigma Theta Tau International Foundation of Nursing – The Foundation holds all permanent funds of the honor society. These assets are distributed over nine different endowed or restricted funds, each established for a specific purpose. Endowed funds contain donations made by members and friends of nursing, but only the interest earned from these funds are distributed. Restricted funds hold monies that are given to the honor society for a specific activity and distributed accordingly.

The International Academic Nursing Alliance –The International Academic Nursing Alliance (IANA) is a global electronic community of academicians in nursing united by common professional ideals and goals and a culture of caring, committed to scholarly learning and sharing. The vision of IANA is to create a globally inclusive community of nurse educators and scholars who lead by using technology, collaboration and knowledge to influence nursing education, practice and health care.

MISSION

The Honor Society of Nursing, Sigma Theta Tau International provides leadership and scholarship in practice, education and research to enhance the health of all people. We support the learning and professional development of our members who strive to improve nursing care worldwide.

VISION

All five organizations – the Honor Society of Nursing, Sigma Theta Tau International; Nursing Knowledge International; The International Honor Society of Nursing Building Corporation; the Sigma Theta Tau International Foundation for Nursing; and the International Academic Nursing Alliance – exist to further the vision of the honor society, which is to create a global community of nurses who lead using scholarship, knowledge and technology to improve the health of the world's people.

MEMBERSHIP

Membership is by invitation to baccalaureate and graduate nursing students who demonstrate excellence in scholarship, and to nurse leaders exhibiting exceptional achievements in nursing. Here are some additional facts about our membership:

- More than 360,000 members have been inducted worldwide.

- More than 125,000 active members make Sigma Theta Tau International the second largest nursing organization in the world.

- Members reside in more than 90 countries.

- Sixty-one percent of active members hold master's and/or doctoral degrees. Forty-eight percent are clinicians, 21 percent are administrators or supervisors and 20 percent are educators or researchers.

- There are 431 chapters on 515 college campuses in Australia, Botzwana, Brazil, Canada, Hong Kong, Mexico, the Netherlands, Pakistan, South Africa, South Korea, Swaziland, Taiwan, Tanzania and the U.S.

The honor society communicates regularly with more than 100 nurse leaders who have expressed interest in establishing a chapter in other countries and territories, including Chile, China, Colombia, Costa Rica, Denmark, Finland, India, Iran, Ireland, Israel, Germany, Japan, Jamaica, Lebanon, Lithuania, New Zealand, Spain, Sweden, Thailand and the United Kingdom.

PRODUCTS AND SERVICES

From its inception, the honor society has recognized the value of scholarship and excellence in nursing practice. In 1936 the honor society became the first U.S. organization to fund nursing research. Today, the honor society supports these values through its numerous professional development products and services that focus on the core areas of education, leadership, career development, evidence-based nursing, research and scholarship. These products and services advance the learning and professional development of members and all nurses who strive to improve the health of the world's people:

- The honor society, with its chapters and grant partners (corporations, associations and foundations), contributes more than $650,000 annually to nursing research through grants, scholarships and monetary awards.

- A number of education and research conferences are supported by the honor society, including a yearly research congress that presents the latest nursing research from around the world and a biennial convention that offers nursing's best practices in clinical, scientific and leadership areas.

- Online continuing education offers peer-reviewed, interactive learning activities which are presented in a variety of learning formats including case studies, evidence-based articles and module courses. These activities are Web-linked to full-text articles and abstracts and are available for continuing education contact hours.

- CareerMap, the honor society's career development service, provides resources for every stage in the career process, from selection of nursing as a profession to active retirement.

- Leadership programs include mentoring programs and global health care think tanks.

The honor society produces a variety of publications that also support the learning and professional development of nurses:

- *Journal of Nursing Scholarship,* a leading, peer-reviewed scholarly journal with a global circulation of 120,000, is published quarterly and is available in both print and full-text, searchable online formats to members and subscribers.

- *Reflections on Nursing Leadership* is the honor society's award-winning, full-color quarterly newsmagazine that communicates nurses' contributions and relevance to the health of people worldwide.

- *Worldviews on Evidence-Based Nursing*™, a quarterly periodical available in print and full text, searchable online formats to members and subscribers, is a leading global source of the best research and evidence available with applications to nursing practice, administration, education and policy.

- *Excellence in Nursing Knowledge* is a monthly member newsletter that introduces readers to best practices and evidence-driven processes from multiple perspectives in different institutions. Each issue includes multi-faceted content of interest to nurses in clinical, administrative and educational settings.

- *Chapter Leader Emphasis* is a quarterly newsletter sent to more than 4,500 chapter leaders.

- *Create the Future Through Renewal* is a monthly electronic newsletter sent to all members.

- Scholarly books on a wide range of topics in nursing and health care of interest to members and other nurses around the world.

In addition, the honor society houses the Virginia Henderson International Nursing Library, a premier, online library offering these services and resources:

- A collection of more than 17,000 nursing research studies, as well as researchers' demographic information and study abstracts. It also contains abstracts from major nursing research conferences, including research events sponsored by the honor society.

- A comprehensive, advanced search function to access library resources.

Presidents

1. 1929-34   Dorothy Ford Buschmann, Alpha,(deceased)
2. 1934-38   Florence Parisa, Delta, (deceased)
3. 1938-41   Ruth P. Kuehn, Epsilon, (deceased, died November 1986)
4. 1941-47   Katharine J. Densford Dreves, Zeta, (died 28 September 1978)
5. 1947-51   Frances L. George Steward, Eta
6. 1951-55   Thelma Dodds, Zeta, (deceased; reported in Spring, 1990 Reflections)
7. 1955-57   Myrtle Kitchell Aydelotte, RN, PhD, FAAN; Gamma
8. 1957-59   Dr. Lois M. Austin, Epsilon, (deceased, died Spring, 1986)
9. 1959-62   Edna H. Treasure Whitley, Kappa, (died in 1991)
10. 1962-65   Dr. Catherine McClure, Eta (deceased, died 28 January 2001)
11. 1965-71   Virginia Crenshaw, RN, MPH, EdD; Iota
12. 1971-75   Ruth Hepler, PhD; Alpha Epsilon
13. 1975-81   Sr. Rosemary Donley, SC, PhD, APRN, BC, FAAN; Eta
14. 1981-83   Carol Lindeman, RN, PHD, FAAN; Beta Psi
15. 1983-85   Lucie Young Kelly, RN, PhD, FAAN; Alpha Zeta
16. 1985-87   Ms. Vernice D. Ferguson, RN, MA, FAAN, FRCN; Kappa
17. 1987-89   Angela Barron McBride, RN, PhD, FAAN; Alpha
18. 1989-91   Billye J. Brown, RN, EdD, FAAN; Epsilon Theta
19. 1991-93   Beth Vaughan-Wrobel, RN, EdD, FAAN; Beta Beta and Gamma Xi
20. 1993-95   Fay L. Bower, RN, DNSc, FAAN; Alpha Gamma and Beta Gamma
21. 1995-97   Melanie C. Dreher, RN, PhD, FAAN; Beta Zeta
22. 1997-99   Eleanor J. Sullivan, RN, PhD, FAAN; Delta and Delta Lambda
23. 1999-2001   Patricia E. Thompson, RN, EdD, FAAN; Beta Chi and Gamma Xi
24. 2001-2003   May L. Wykle, RN, PhD, FAAN; Alpha Mu
25. 2003-2005   Daniel J. Pesut, PhD, APRN, BC, FAAN; Alpha
26. 2005-2007   Carol Picard, RN, PhD, CS; Alpha Chi, Beta Zeta-at-large, and Epsilon Beta

Member Data

Convention Themes

2005	Create the Future Through Renewal (38th)
2003	Building Diverse Relationships
2001	Learning and Leading Globally (36th)
1999	Avenues into the Future (35th)
1997	Celebrating 75 Years of Excellence (34th)
1995	Celebrating a New Era (33rd)
1993	The Leadership Challenge (32nd)
1991	Creating Nursing's Future (31st)
1989	A Distinguished Past-A Dynamic Future (30th)
1987	Celebrate Worldwide Nursing Scholarship (29th)
1985	Focus on the Public (28th)
1983	Image Makers: Richness & Diversity (27th)
1981	Scholars in Action (26th)
1979	Leadership in Action (25th)
1977	Leadership in Action (24th)
1975	Sigma Theta Tau in Action (23rd)

Chapter Charters

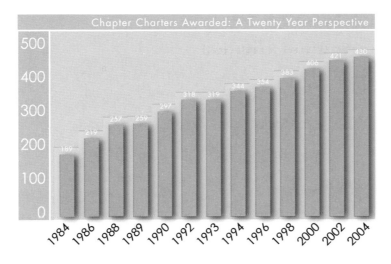

Chapter Charters Awarded: A Twenty Year Perspective

YEAR	NUMBER OF CHARTERS	TOTAL NUMBER OF CHARTERS	YEAR	NUMBER OF CHARTERS	TOTAL NUMBER OF CHARTERS
1922	1	1	1978	18	94
1929	1	2	1979	1	95
1931	1	3	1980	33	128
1934	1	4	1981	1	129
1946	1	5	1982	31	160
1953	4	9	1983	1	161
1955	1	10	1984	28	189
1958	2	12	1986	30	219
1959	3	15	1988	38	257
1960	1	16	1989	2	259
1961	2	18	1990	38	297
1962	4	22	1992	21	318
1963	3	25	1993	1	319
1964	5	30	1994	25	344
1966	9	39	1996	10	354
1968	2	41	1998	29	383
1970	9	50	2000	23	406
1972	6	56	2002	18	421
1974	9	65	2004	12	430*
1976	11	76			

*Several dissolutions leads to the number not equaling 421 + 12

Membership Active Counts

DATE	NUMBER OF MEMBERS	DATE	NUMBER OF MEMBERS
Sep-75	15,200	Nov-01	111,142
Sep-76	19,500	Dec-01	112,107
Sep-77	22,800	Jan-02	112,483
Sep-78	26,750	Feb-02	112,433
Sep-79	28,300	Mar-02	111,092
Sep-80	35,100	Apr-02	115,276
Sep-81	39,500	May-02	120,921
Sep-82	46,000	Jun-02	122,524
Sep-83	51,560	Jul-02	121,360
Sep-84	59,070	Aug-02	116,862
Sep-85	63,460	Sep-02	113,823
Sep-86	70,537	Oct-02	112,742
Sep-87	74,460	Nov-02	112,050
Sep-88	82,187	Dec-02	114,319
Sep-89	85,540	Jan-03	113,913
Sep-90	92,764	Feb-03	113,325
Sep-91	95,124	Mar-03	111,848
Sep-92	100,710	Apr-03	116,308
Sep-93	106,063	May-03	120,995
Sep-94	113,776	Jun-03	121,754
Sep-95	115,906	Jul-03	121,993
Sep-96	118,368	Aug-03	117,154
Sep-97	123,426	Sep-03	114,308
Sep-98	114,602	Oct-03	114,098
Jul-99	118,651	Nov-03	113,800
Oct-99	121,681	Dec-03	114,680
Feb-00	110,582	Jan-04	116,555
Mar-00	111,213	Feb-04	115,758
Apr-00	120,598	Mar-04	115,030
May-00	121,596	Apr-04	115,735
Jun-00	115,581	May-04	122,906
Jul-00	113,512	Jun-04	124,918
Aug-00	119,179	Jul-04	125,447
Sep-00	109,133	Aug-04	120,409
Dec-00	110,855	Sep-04	117,764
Feb-01	109,738	Oct-04	116,901
Mar-01	111,802	Nov-04	117,545
Apr-01	110,820	Dec-04	117,172
May-01	118,583	Jan-05	117,965
Jun-01	117,963	Feb-05	117,352
Jul-01	112,549	Mar-05	118,851
Aug-01	110,542	Apr-05	124,912
Sep-01	111,942	May-05	127,069
Oct-01	112,153	Jun-05	128,522

References

Aydelotte, M.K. (1976). *Reflections, 2*(1), 3-6.

Barnsteiner, J. (1993). The Online Journal of Knowledge Synthesis for Nursing. *Reflections, 19*(1), 8.

Blinkenlights Archaeological Institute. (1999-2002). *What was the first personal computer?* Retrieved October 19, 2005, from http://www.blinkenlights.com/pc.shtml

The dedication. (1989a). *Reflections, 15*(4), 1.

The dedication. (1989b). *Reflections, 15*(4), 1.

The dedication. (1989c). *Reflections, 15*(4), 1.

Donley, R. (1978). Vision for the future. *Reflections, 4*(1), 1.

Ferguson, V. (1986). President's message: Our recipe for success. *Reflections, (12)*3, 3.

Fondiller, S.H. (1993). Vernice Ferguson: Scholar at large. *Reflections, (20)*2, 5.

Houser, B., & Player, K. 2004. *Pivotal moments in nursing: Leaders who changed the path of nursing.* Indianapolis, IN: Sigma Theta Tau International.

IBM. (n.d.). *IBM 5510 portable computer.* Retrieved October 19, 2005, from http://www-03.ibm.com/ibm/history/exhibits/pc/pc_2.html

Kelly, L.S. (1987). A letter to all members. *Reflections, 13*(1), 6.

Pesut, D. (2004). From the president. *Reflections on Nursing Leadership, 30*(1), 57.

Strategic Plan 2005. (2000). *Reflections on Nursing Leadership, 26*(1), 55-62.

Vinas, M. S. (1999). *Chronology of medical/technological advances.* Retrieved October 19, 2005, from http://perfline.com/textbook/local/mvinas_chronol.htm#20THb

Watts, N. (1979). A salute to nursing contributors. *Reflections, 5*(1), 2.

Why a building fund? (1980). *Reflections, 6*(2), 8.

Wikipedia. (2005a). *Nobel Prize in physiology or medicine.* Retrieved October 19, 2005, from http://en.wikipedia.org/wiki/Nobel_Prize_in_Physiology_or_Medicine

Wikipedia. (2005b). *World population.* Retrieved October 19, 2005, from http://en.wikipedia.org/wiki/World_population

World Health Organization. (2003). *HIV/AIDS: Confronting a killer.* Retrieved October 19, 2005, from http://www.who.int/whr/2003/en/Chapter3.pdf

World Health Organization. (2005). *Epidemic and pandemic alert and response.* Retrieved October 19, 2005, from http://www.who.int/csr/disease/smallpox/en/

Writers' seminar a great success. (1978). *Reflections, 4*(2), 8.

Wykle, M. (2002). Letter from the president. *Reflections on Nursing Leadership, 28*(1), 51.